The History of England

An Enthralling Overview of English History

© Copyright 2024 - All rights reserved.

The content contained within this book may not be reproduced, duplicated, or transmitted without direct written permission from the author or the publisher.

Under no circumstances will any blame or legal responsibility be held against the publisher, or author, for any damages, reparation, or monetary loss due to the information contained within this book, either directly or indirectly.

Legal Notice:

This book is copyright protected. It is only for personal use. You cannot amend, distribute, sell, use, quote, or paraphrase any part, or the content within this book, without the consent of the author or publisher.

Disclaimer Notice:

Please note the information contained within this document is for educational and entertainment purposes only. All effort has been executed to present accurate, up-to-date, reliable, and complete information. No warranties of any kind are declared or implied. Readers acknowledge that the author is not engaging in the rendering of legal, financial, medical, or professional advice. The content within this book has been derived from various sources. Please consult a licensed professional before attempting any techniques outlined in this book.

By reading this document, the reader agrees that under no circumstances is the author responsible for any losses, direct or indirect, that are incurred as a result of the use of the information contained within this document, including, but not limited to, errors, omissions, or inaccuracies.

Free limited time bonus

Stop for a moment. We have a free bonus set up for you. The problem is this: we forget 90% of everything that we read after 7 days. Crazy fact, right? Here's the solution: we've created a printable, 1-page pdf summary for this book that you're reading now. All you have to do to get your free pdf summary is to go to the following website:

https://livetolearn.lpages.co/enthrallinghistory/

Or, Scan the QR code!

Once you do, it will be intuitive. Enjoy, and thank you!

Table of Contents

INTRODUCTION 1
CHAPTER 1: PREHISTORY AND THE BRONZE AGE 2
CHAPTER 2: THE CELTS 10
CHAPTER 3: ROMAN BRITAIN 19
CHAPTER 4: THE ANGLO-SAXONS 28
CHAPTER 5: THE VIKING RAIDS AND THE FORMATION OF ENGLAND 36
CHAPTER 6: THE NORMAN CONQUEST 45
CHAPTER 7: THE PLANTAGENETS 52
CHAPTER 8: THE HUNDRED YEARS' WAR AND THE BLACK DEATH 62
CHAPTER 9: THE WARS OF THE ROSES 70
CHAPTER 10: THE TUDORS AND THE ENGLISH REFORMATION 79
CHAPTER 11: ELIZABETH I 87
CHAPTER 12: THE STUARTS 95
CHAPTER 13: THE CIVIL WARS AND THE PROTECTORATE 103
CHAPTER 14: RESTORATION AND THE UNION WITH SCOTLAND 110
CHAPTER 15: EIGHTEENTH-CENTURY BRITAIN: EXPANSION, WARS, AND REVOLUTIONS 119
CHAPTER 16: THE UNION WITH IRELAND 127

CHAPTER 17: THE VICTORIAN ERA	136
CHAPTER 18: WORLD WAR I AND II	144
CONCLUSION	152
HERE'S ANOTHER BOOK BY ENTHRALLING HISTORY THAT YOU MIGHT LIKE	155
FREE LIMITED TIME BONUS	156
BIBLIOGRAPHY	157

Introduction

The history of England is an enormous topic that we will discover has neither a set beginning nor end. From its origins as a nation to its presence in the modern day, enough has happened in England's history to fill countless volumes.

To discuss all those events is not possible, nor is it the goal of this book. The process of writing any history, and most especially the history of an entire country, inevitably requires that some things fall by the wayside. Therefore, this book seeks to give an overall picture of the major events that shaped the emergence of England as a nation and its growth and development. In these pages, you will learn things like who lived in England before the English, how England was formed, how its government developed, how the British Empire formed, and more.

What you won't find here are extensive biographies of every monarch or a detailed explanation of every major battle. While there will be plenty of interesting facts and fascinating details throughout, this book aims to be comprehensive rather than all-encompassing. It's an easy-to-understand guide to a long and complex topic. By the time you finish, you will have a working knowledge of the entire history of England!

Whether you are interested in the Roman Empire, Vikings, warfare, politics, kings and queens, exploration, or something else entirely, there's something in England's storied history for you. So, let's dive into the story of a nation that started on a small island and went on to profoundly impact the entire globe.

Chapter 1: Prehistory and the Bronze Age

Where does history start? If we are setting out on a tour of the history of England, where should we begin? The question of where to start history may sound philosophical, but it tends to be answered practically. We may believe that the history of England began with the beginning of time itself, but we will find ourselves extremely limited in our ability to discuss this because of a lack of information. For the historian, then, history begins with information—but what information, exactly? Information comes in many different forms, but the type of information we specifically use to define history is the written record. When written records begin, so does history.

Of course, there are problems with this approach. For one, records came into existence at vastly different times in various parts of the world. This means history starts at different times depending on where you are. The other problem is larger. Civilization doesn't necessarily start with writing. Many groups developed sophisticated cultures based on oral traditions.

If we begin history with the written record, what do we do with all the people and things that happened before written records appeared in a particular area? The answer is deceptively simple. We just don't call it history. Prehistory is the study of the past before written records. It does not mean the people living in this time were primitive or that not much was happening. It does mean we don't know as much about this time and are often forced to speculate about what we know.

Historians like written records because they are clear. Even when they are biased and misleading, written records offer clarity that makes piecing together the story of the past plausible. When looking at prehistory, we are forced to rely on very different sources. Archaeologists are the experts of prehistory. The burial sites, monuments, and relics of the past are all we have to complete the puzzle of what was happening before anyone started writing things down.

As we mentioned earlier, various cultures started using writing at different times. So, looking specifically at the history of England, when was that? For England, history starts in 43 CE with the Roman conquest, which brought the Latin language and writing. Technically, you could push this date back about a century to 55 BCE with Julius Caesar's *Commentaries on the Gallic Wars.* This is the first written description we have of Britain.

Even if we start with 55 BCE, that still leaves a lot of English prehistory to cover. Who did the Romans conquer? Who was living in England (otherwise known as Britain) before 43 CE, and what were they like? In the first two chapters of this book, we will cover the enormous time span that makes up Britain's prehistory before the Roman invasion.

Prehistory is typically divided into three main eras: the Stone Age, Bronze Age, and Iron Age, named for the materials that humans at that time used to fashion tools, weapons, and other objects. In this chapter, we will be taking a tour of the Stone and Bronze Ages.

The Stone Age

History begins with information, and prehistory is the same way, so what information do we have about the very beginnings of Britain? As you might suspect, the answer is not much. We know very little about the period referred to as the Stone Age, which covers roughly 800,000 BCE to 2000 BCE. Since it covers such a massive amount of time, the Stone Age is further subdivided into the Paleolithic, Mesolithic, and Neolithic eras, which mean Old, Middle, and New Stone Ages, respectively.

The Paleolithic era was not a happening time in Britain. It lasted from around 800,000 BCE to 10,000 BCE. This was the time of the Ice Age, and Britain's northern location meant that for large chunks of time, the island was uninhabitable for humans. However, "island" is not the right word to use, as it is believed that Britain was a peninsula connected to mainland Europe. Britain's connection to Europe is what allowed humans to travel there in the first place, but the extreme cold of the Ice Age prevented Britain from becoming a major hub of human activity in this period.

By the Mesolithic era, which lasted from around 10,000 BCE to 4000 BCE, things had started to warm up—so much so that sea levels rose and Britain began its existence as an island. With warmer temperatures, the island could sustain far more life. The humans who lived in Britain in the Mesolithic era were hunter-gatherers. They often moved with the seasons, following their food sources, but there is also evidence of small settlements.

Around 4000 BCE, farming came to the shores of England, and the Neolithic era began. The Neolithic era lasted from about 4000 BCE to 2000 BCE. It is thought that farming came to Britain through people migrating from the continent.

Farming had a profound impact on Britain and its people because it allowed a settled lifestyle that was impossible when people had to follow their food sources around. In the Neolithic era, we thus see an increase in the number of settlements.

Farming also causes humans to interact differently with their environment. Forests were cleared to make room for fields and pastures. The more permanent nature of farming communities also led to the construction of barrows and other monuments. With farming, humans were, for the first time, bending their environment to their will. They were still at the mercy of Mother Nature, but now that they were settling in one place, they had time to build. The Neolithic era witnessed the construction of stone circles, henges, mounds, and more. Stonehenge was built toward the end of the Neolithic age. We will discuss these mysterious monuments in more detail later in the chapter.

That's the gist of the Stone Age. England moved from being a frozen chunk connected to mainland Europe to an island with hunter-gatherers and then farmers.

The Bronze Age

In roughly 2000 BCE, metalworking arrived in Britain and began the period known as the Bronze Age. Metalworking began with copper and gold, but bronze (an alloy of copper and tin) is harder. By 2200 BCE, it was the metal of choice for making tools and weapons.

What we know about the Bronze Age is based on what managed to survive long enough for us to find it. This means we know a lot about burial practices because many graves from this era remained undisturbed. In the early Bronze Age, people in Britain buried their dead under barrows (shaped mounds of earth). These barrows and the graves they covered were often placed near other constructions like Stonehenge, creating large areas that appear to have been for solely ceremonial purposes.

A photograph of Stonehenge, Wiltshire, England in 2011.
Tristan J. Wilson, CC0, via Wikimedia Commons:
https://commons.wikimedia.org/wiki/File:TJDW_Stonehenge_20111107.tif

Another interesting thing to note about the barrows is that this is the first time we see large individual graves in Britain. The dead in these barrows were often buried with grave goods, as well. The fact that Bronze Age people took the time to build elaborate constructions for certain graves shows that some people were viewed as more important than others, indicating the establishment of a social hierarchy. Later in the period, cremation became more common, and our knowledge of burial practices dwindles through the remainder of the Bronze Age.

Other information we have gleaned about the Bronze Age through archaeological findings relates to the living rather than the dead. We know that roundhouses, which were round, single-room dwellings with a thatched roof, appeared in this era. We also see small groupings of houses, indicating the establishment of communities, and the earliest construction of hillforts, which suggests that warfare between rival communities had also begun. During this period, there was even trade with the continent, especially in metal.

With communities came other aspects of human society, such as hierarchies, warfare, and trade. Once humans in Britain began to settle down, they quickly began to acquire land and goods, and with this came the basic problem of economics: scarcity. There are not infinite resources, so inevitably some people have more than others. This results in social elites—those who have more—and warfare, as groups resort to taking what they don't have. Trade also emerges as a way of gaining resources that are not easily accessible.

Trade, hierarchy, and warfare existed in the Stone Age, but they began to increase in the Bronze Age as farming increased populations and created a surplus of time and resources. When the Bronze Age ended and the Iron Age began around 800 BCE, the importance of these aspects of human society in Britain only increased.

Stonehenge and Other Constructions

One of the most fascinating aspects of Britain's prehistory is easily the mysterious stone circles built during the period, many of which remain standing to this day. How and why did prehistoric peoples construct these massive monuments?

Stonehenge, located in southwest England, is by far the most famous of Britain's remaining stone circles. Before we go any further, let's answer the pressing question and admit that we don't know why Stonehenge was built. There are myriads of theories. Some say Stonehenge was part of druid rituals (although this is highly unlikely because Stonehenge predates the druids). Others believe it to be an ancient calendar since it is perfectly aligned with the movement of the sun. It could also be a monument to the dead, a gathering place, or a place of healing. In short, we don't know.

There's more to the mystery of Stonehenge besides its purpose, though. Another pressing question is just how prehistoric peoples managed to build it. Stonehenge was constructed over hundreds of years beginning in the Neolithic era around 3000 BCE and ending in the Bronze Age around 1500 BCE. The monument includes far more than just the central stone circle. It is surrounded by a circular earthwork henge, including two round barrows to the north and south and many others nearby. A series of holes surround the monument, and a few solitary stones are carefully positioned in relation to the movement of the sun. The Stonehenge area thus appears to be a sacred site rather than just a singular monument.

The idea that there is something special about the location of Stonehenge is furthered by the effort it undoubtedly took to get the stones to that location. Stonehenge consists of two types of stones: sarsen stones and bluestones. The sarsen stones are the large, shaped stones that make the post-and-lintel (two stones forming pillars with a stone on top) parts of the monument, and the bluestones are the smaller stones. Bluestones are only found in South Wales, which is over a hundred miles away from Stonehenge. Something was special enough about that location to make prehistoric people find a way to lug those enormous stones hundreds of miles.

There's a lot we don't know about Stonehenge, and the mystery is part of the fun. However, Stonehenge is also important for what it tells us about the people of prehistoric Britain. We know that they were capable of planning and executing projects that took many generations and a lot of manpower. We know they must have had some engineering knowledge because they could raise and place the stones. We know they had advanced astronomical knowledge because it is aligned with the movement of the sun. What Stonehenge tells us is that Britain's prehistoric people were far more advanced than the stereotypical cavemen we might be tempted to picture.

Of course, while it is the most famous, Stonehenge is far from the only stone circle or monument dating to Britain's prehistoric era. There are many stone circles scattered around Britain. This seems to indicate a large degree of shared culture across the island. But, since we don't know what the stone circles were used for, it is difficult to draw many conclusions about what the culture was like.

Stone circles are not the only large building projects from this period. Large tombs, hillforts, and earthwork henges and barrows are all evidence of this society's construction capabilities. These extensive building projects show us that by 3000 BCE and beyond, humans in Britain had figured out how to survive well enough to have time for building things for ceremonial and sacred importance. Even from our earliest history, humans have felt a drive to go beyond survival.

Piecing Together Prehistory

As mentioned and observed, what we know about prehistory comes from what people left behind. This means that while we know a lot about what prehistoric people had, trying to figure out why they had it and how they used it is a trickier task. How do we piece together the puzzle of prehistory from the remnants that remain today?

Butser Ancient Farm is a place in present-day England that is trying new ways to answer this question. The farm is an experimental archaeological site and open-air museum where reconstructions of ancient-style houses and farms are created. The researchers at Butser Ancient Farm recreated these buildings using the same tools prehistoric peoples had access to. They also make weapons, plant crops, take care of animals, and more, all using only the tools ancient people would have had.

Besides giving visitors a chance to see what prehistoric life might have looked like, the research at Butser Ancient Farm is crucial to examining how prehistoric peoples might have lived. By doing the same tasks with the same tools, researchers can at least begin to answer the question of how people lived. For example, researchers have established that it was possible to pull plows from the era using cows and produce enough grain to have a surplus for export using the agricultural techniques of the day. Of course, all these experiments can establish is plausibility, but plausibility gives us a much clearer picture of prehistoric life than we previously had.

What remains elusive about the prehistoric age is religion and culture. This was a period of oral traditions, which unfortunately means we know virtually nothing about what these people believed. We don't know why they built Stonehenge and other stone circles, what stories they told each other, what gods they believed in, or how they worshiped. Technically, we don't even know if they had gods or a form of worship.

Not knowing things for sure does not mean we cannot speculate based on archaeological findings, however. The discovery of a mummified body in the bogs of northwest England led to such speculation. Lindow Man, as the body was dubbed, was found in 1984. The body was that of a young man, and all that was left was a head, torso, and foot. He died sometime near the end of the Iron Age.

Lindow Man is puzzling because of the excessive violence that apparently caused his death. A garrote was around his neck, he had suffered blows to the head, and he had been stabbed. Any one of these three things would have killed him, so the multiple causes of death have led many to speculate that there was something more ritualistic about Lindow Man's death than plain murder. Some believe this was part of an elaborate execution. Others think Lindow Man may have been a religious sacrifice, perhaps even a willing one as his remains show no signs of a struggle.

Lindow Man and Butser Ancient Farm are both examples of how our knowledge of British prehistory continues to grow. Discoveries are still being made, and as we gather new information, we are forced to reevaluate our assumptions, leading to new speculations and conclusions about this era. The far reaches of Britain's past remain mysterious, but continuous research has allowed us to have a general idea of Britain's human beginnings.

Chapter 2: The Celts

Who were the first Britons? So far, we have simply referred to the people living on the island as the people in Britain, but who were they? The very first Britons don't have a name. We know they came from the continent, but the part of the continent they came from and who exactly they were remains a mystery. In the Stone and Bronze Ages, large tribes had yet to form. The people who migrated from the mainland of Europe to the British Isles were a disparate group we cannot lump together into a single identity.

The first group to settle in Britain that we assign a name to are the Celts. Celtic people and Celtic culture dominated Britain through the Iron Age and the arrival of the Romans, and their impact in the region can still be seen today, particularly in Cornwall, Scotland, and Wales, where Celtic languages are still spoken. But who exactly were the Celts? Where did they come from, and what were they like?

Who Were the Celts?

Map of Iron Age Britain.
Ulysses1975, CC BY-SA 3.0 <https://creativecommons.org/licenses/by-sa/3.0>, via Wikimedia Commons: https://commons.wikimedia.org/wiki/File:Map_-_Peoples_of_Britain_and_Ireland_100BCE.JPG

The Celts are a somewhat difficult group to define, largely because they are not a single group. The first archaeological evidence of the Celts' existence appears in central Europe, where they traded with the Greeks. In fact, the word "Celt" comes from the Greek word *Keltoi*, which means "barbarian."

The Greeks believed that they were the only civilized culture. Since they tended to view all foreigners as barbarians, the word "Celt" is a rather broad term that refers to the entire group of varying tribes and clans of central Europe. The Celts likely saw themselves as disparate groups, but in the eyes of outsiders, like the Greeks, the culture and appearance of the tribes were close enough to lump them all together.

From central Europe, the Celts spread westward and eastward, eventually reaching as far west as Spain and the British Isles. As the Celts spread to different areas and were made up of different tribes, they acquired different names. The Celts who settled in the area that became modern-day France were known as the Gauls. Those who settled in Ireland and Scotland were the Gaels (from which the Gaelic languages are derived), and the Celts who settled in what would become modern-day England and Wales were the Britons.

Like the name "Celt," the subdivisions "Gauls," "Gaels," and "Britons" were assigned to the Celtic tribes by outsiders. The Britons, for instance, consisted of several different Celtic tribes, such as the Iceni and the Belgae. The name "Briton" is derived from the name the Greek explorer Pytheas gave the islands. Pytheas called the islands "Pretannike," from the Celtic word *Pretani*, which means "painted people." It is unclear if this is what the Celts called themselves, it was a name for a particular group, or something else. The *p* eventually changed to a *b*, and by the time of the Roman conquests, the Romans were calling the island "Britannia." The tribes living there were dubbed "Britons."

What does all this information about names have to do with understanding who the Celts were, though? For one, it is helpful to clarify that the term "Celtic" refers to many different groups (Britons, Gauls, Gaels, and more). Secondly, these groups were named by outsiders and did not see themselves as a single entity. The various tribes fought each other. The Celts spread and dominated Europe in the Iron Age, but they were not an empire in the sense that Rome would soon become. Finally, knowing the origin of some of these names teaches us the surprising fact that the Britons were not the original inhabitants of Britain. They were the

Celtic tribes that migrated to the island of Britain in the Iron Age. They were technically invaders just like the Romans, Anglo-Saxons, Vikings, and Normans that would come after them. England is, if nothing else, a land settled by outsiders.

You may be wondering, then, if the Celts were made up of different tribes, why we bother talking about them as a group. The Celts shared several commonalities in their culture that make it worth discussing them collectively.

Celtic Culture

Despite being made up of many warring tribes, the Celts shared a language, religious practices, art style, and other things that make a discussion of Celtic culture both possible and informative.

Perhaps the largest factor uniting the various tribes that made up the Celts was language. This does not mean that all the Celtic tribes across Europe in the Iron Age spoke the same language. Rather, their languages are all derived from a common source (Celtic). All the groups likely began speaking a common version of Celtic, but as they migrated and spread, the language evolved into different languages with a shared root.

The Celtic languages can be divided into two major groups: those spoken on the continent and those spoken on the British Isles. Unfortunately, we know little about the continental Celtic languages as these languages became extinct and we have few, if any, surviving examples of them. Perhaps because of their isolation, the Celtic languages of the British Isles survived far better. These languages include the British Celtic languages (derived from the Brittonic language used in the Iron Age and Roman period) of Welsh, Cornish, and Breton, and the Goidelic languages of Irish, Scottish Gaelic, and Manx. In the continued existence of these Celtic languages, we can see the perseverance of Celtic culture. This was the first group to inhabit Britain that would become an essential part of England's cultural heritage.

Another shared aspect of Celtic culture was religious beliefs. The Celts did not regularly build temples or statues of their gods, but they showed a belief in the sacred and the afterlife. Celts gave offerings and sacrifices to gods and believed that certain spaces, such as particular groves and springs, were sacred. They also buried their dead with objects, which is typical of cultures that believe in some sort of afterlife.

Besides these general characteristics, we don't know much about Celtic religious practices and beliefs because this aspect of Celtic life was overseen by the druids. Druids were the priest class of Celtic society who played a large role in life beyond religion. They were the tribe historians who acted as ambassadors, judges, and more. However, unfortunately for modern historians, the druids guarded their knowledge and secrets carefully. What they did pass on was through oral tradition. This means we now have essentially nothing left to tell us more about the druids and Celtic religious practices. We do know that the druids were quite the headache for the Romans later, and it is presumed that as leaders of their people, the druids were often behind uprisings against Roman rule.

What else do we know about Celtic culture? Although the Romans and Greeks viewed the Celts as barbarians, they had a sophisticated culture. While Greco-Roman artwork of the period was focused on clean lines and realism, Celtic art was more abstract and flowing. The Celts focused heavily on animal figures, and much of their art is decorating practical objects such as shields, pottery, and brooches.

One object peculiar to this period that Celts often wore and could make quite ornate was the torc. Torcs were rigid, metal necklaces that typically opened in the front. Torcs were not unique to the Celts. They were worn by other groups at this time, but they appear to have been particularly important to the Celts. Celtic torcs were often made of gold and appear to have been a sign of wealth and status. They may also have been connected with the spiritual realm, as Celtic gods were often depicted wearing torcs. Their importance to Celtic culture means that torcs are commonly associated with the Celts.

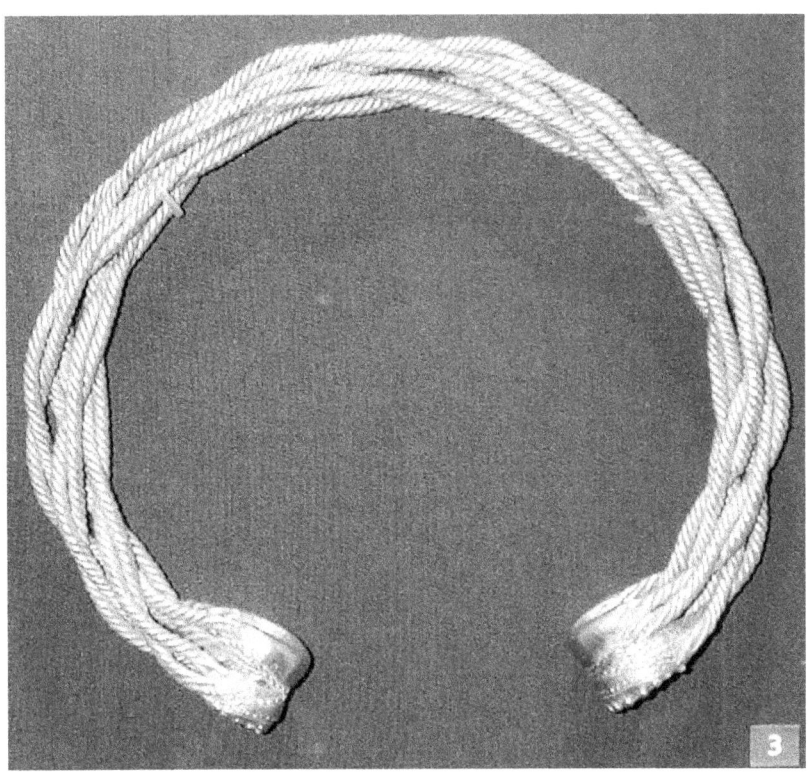
Iron Age Torc from the British Museum.
https://commons.wikimedia.org/wiki/File:IronAgeTorcBritishMuseum.JPG

So, even though the Celts were far from being a unified nation, they had many similarities that make it possible for us to discuss Celtic culture. Although they did not have a written tradition, the Celts had a sophisticated culture with their own art style, religion, and language. Unfortunately, because of the lack of written records, we do not know as much as we would like about Celtic culture, particularly the druids.

Celtic Society

Culture is not the only thing that makes the Celts unique. There are other aspects of Celtic society to consider, such as structure and economics. Celtic society, like most societies, was hierarchical. At the top of the hierarchy were the warriors. If you could protect your people and successfully take stuff from your neighbor, you got to be in charge. The religious leaders, druids, were also in the top echelon of society. Under the warrior aristocracy and druids were those with specialized skills and jobs such as poets, craftsmen, and traders. Beneath this group were the farmers and the enslaved. Most of the population would have been at the bottom of the hierarchy. However, it appears that movement between social classes (except for the enslaved) was possible if one acquired enough wealth.

Shockingly, gender does not appear to have been a major factor in the hierarchy of Celtic society. Women could own property and choose their husbands, and they could even rule, as evidenced by the famous queen of the Iceni, Boudicca. There is also evidence that Celtic women fought alongside the men.

This hierarchical society was broken into tribes, which might have been led by a monarch or an elected chief. Kinship was important for the ruling elite of Celtic society. It was crucial to maintaining control because the Celts lacked writing in the Iron Age. A single king could not effectively rule a large area because there was no way to issue laws, make decrees, and ensure uniformity across his realm. However, a king could give control of land to his brother or cousin. One way these alliances were formed was by fostering children with other families. The result of all this was that the elites of Celtic society were a web of extended families using kinship to consolidate control.

So, that's how Celtic society was organized, but what did the Celts do in their society? To outsiders, the Celts were seen as fierce warriors. They were known for charging into battle naked and covered in paint, which was terrifying for their enemies. They might also wear helmets that looked like animals. To add to the terror Celtic warriors inspired, they also often wore the heads of enemies they had killed into battle. Besides being scary enough to make anyone think twice about going head-to-head with them, the Celts wore their enemies' heads because they believed the seat of the soul was in the head. To steal your enemy's head was to steal his essence and his power.

The Celts also favored the use of chariots in battle. They rode on light chariots that allowed them to strike their enemies fast and hard, causing the maximum amount of chaos. Imagine screaming, naked, paint-covered warriors hurtling forward on chariots, and you will begin to see why Celtic warriors were so feared in the ancient world. It is no wonder the Romans had so much trouble subduing the Celtic tribes in their quest to conquer Europe. Eventually, superior organization and resources would allow the Romans to triumph, but the Celts were a thorn in the empire's side for quite a while.

Although they were known for their skill in warfare, the Celts were ultimately farmers, not mercenaries. Farming was how they made their living, and the average Celt spent far more of his time plowing than fighting. It was the Celts who brought the iron plow to Britain, which helped increase agricultural productivity and cultivate more of the island.

While farming was their main occupation, the Celts were not purely subsistence farmers. Their economy thrived enough for them to engage in trade with other cultures. The Celts traded things like enslaved people, furs, and iron for things they could not make themselves, such as wine, silver, and luxury goods like fine pottery.

So, the Celts were farmers who charged into battle naked but also peacefully engaged with other civilizations of the ancient world through trade. This is true of the Celts in general, but what about the Celts specifically living in Britain?

Britain in the Iron Age

The Iron Age lasted from around 800 BCE to the end of British prehistory, which ended with the Roman occupation in 43 CE. This last age of prehistory was dominated by the Celts, who arrived in Britain around 750 BCE at the beginning of the Iron Age. It was the Celts who were responsible for bringing the Iron Age to Britain.

Archaeological evidence shows that the Celts had an advanced knowledge of iron making. Their iron weapons and plows gave them an advantage in warfare and farming. Still, while the Celts in Britain may have been living there during the Iron Age, they did not work exclusively in iron. Iron was the metal of choice for tools and weapons, but the Celts still used bronze and gold to make more decorative items such as torcs.

Like elsewhere, Celtic society in Britain was broken up into tribes, and those tribes often lived in hillforts. While hillforts first appeared in the Bronze Age in Britain, the arrival of the Celts and the Iron Age greatly increased their importance in prehistoric Britain. Hillforts were, as the name suggests, forts built on top of hills. Hillforts were easily defensible because of their high position and additional defensive measures such as ditches and walls. They also tended to be located near essentials like fresh water and to have storage areas within their walls. All of this indicates that these constructions were used as forts for warfare in Celtic society.

The use of hillforts may have extended beyond that, though. Many hillforts contained organized settlements within their walls, and the water sources tended to be located nearby rather than within the walls of the fort. This suggests the hillforts may have been defensible homesteads rather than constructions used solely for warfare.

The extensive number of hillforts in Iron Age Britain tells us quite clearly that the Celts of Britain were not unified. Today, we view Iron Age Britain as a Celtic land, but at the time, it was the home of many different tribes that did not consider themselves Celtic. There were multiple warring tribes, such as the Iceni, the Belgae, the Atrebates, the Brigante, the Catuvellauni, the Parisii, and many more. While they may have been fierce warriors, the Celtic tribes of Britain could not stop fighting among themselves long enough to stand against a bigger threat: the Romans. Although the Celts fought back against Roman rule, they could never gather into a unified front to push the Romans out. By 43 CE, Britain was a Roman province.

Chapter 3: Roman Britain

For Britain, prehistory ends with the Romans. This is not because the Romans were necessarily a more advanced civilization than the Celts but simply because the Romans wrote things down. The first Roman to write about Britain was one of the most famous figures in history, Julius Caesar.

Arrival of the Romans and Conquest

Julius Caesar invaded Britain twice in 55 and 54 BCE. He wrote about the island and his invasions in his book, *The Gallic Wars*. This is the first written record of Britain we still have.

So, why exactly did Julius Caesar invade Britain in the first place? For the Romans, Britain was the island at the edge of the world, at least the edge of the Roman world. It was a remote territory, and the Romans seemed comfortable leaving this island alone until Caesar decided to land there with some legions and cause trouble. Caesar's motivations were likely threefold. One was curiosity. The Romans knew little about Britain. Another reason was closely tied to curiosity, and that was prestige. Because the Romans knew so little about Britain, Caesar being the first to go there and gather information would bolster his reputation. The final reason was more strategic and the actual reason Caesar gives in *The Gallic Wars*.

Starting around 58 BCE, Julius Caesar had been engaged in warfare with the Gauls on the continent. Caesar claimed the Britons were sending aid to the Gauls, so an invasion of the island was necessary to cut off his enemies from their allies. His first invasion in 55 BCE was more of a reconnaissance mission, but in the second invasion in 54 BCE, Caesar's forces engaged with the Britons, led by Cassivellaunus.

Although Caesar's legions ultimately defeated the forces of Cassivellaunus, this was not a conquest. Caesar simply required that Cassivellaunus leave the more pro-Roman king of the Trinovantes, Mandubracius, alone. He then took his legions and went home. This shows that Caesar was not interested in truly conquering Britain. He simply hoped to boost his reputation as a military commander and establish Roman relations with the island. It wasn't until close to 100 years later that Rome would truly conquer Britain.

Rome's conquest of Britain occurred during the reign of Emperor Claudius. Command of the British invasion was given to Aulus Plautius, who was promised governorship of the island if he could successfully conquer Britain for Rome.

Tradition says that the army Plautius gathered for his invasion was none too eager to set sail for Britain. The invasion was held up for months on the Norman coast, and it's easy to see why they were apprehensive. Crossing the English Channel was not easy, and the Roman legions were anything but experienced sailors. Britain was also an entirely unknown land, and the great Julius Caesar had failed to conquer it. No one was pushing to be the first ones to set sail, attempt a rough passage, and land on a hostile shore.

To get his legions moving, Emperor Claudius sent a former slave named Narcissus to take command and represent the emperor. The legions were so offended and shamed at being addressed by a freedman that their fears were replaced by anger, and the invasion finally began in 43 CE.

While the invasion had not gotten off to a promising start, once they landed in Britain, the forces of Aulus Plautius were quite successful. The Roman legions rolled through southeastern Britain with relative ease, annexing territory and setting up client kingdoms wherein Rome controlled external affairs but allowed internal autonomy.

Still, conquering Britain was not an overnight affair for the Romans. Caratacus, chieftain of the Catuvellauni, led resistance to the Romans until his defeat in 51 CE. Southwest England, present-day Wales, was a hotbed of resistance for several decades after the Roman arrival.

To maintain control over the regions they conquered, the Romans established small forts at key positions. While this strategy allowed them to maintain control over a larger area, it left the Roman legions spread too thin to utterly eradicate British resistance. Fighting between the Celtic tribes on the island and the Romans continued for years after Rome's initial conquest in 43 CE. The most famous rebellion to come out of this time was led by the warrior queen of the Iceni, Boudicca.

Boudicca's Rebellion

By 60 CE, the Romans considered the lowlands (south) of Britain conquered. They were pushing north when the seemingly subdued people of the lowlands suddenly erupted in rebellion, led by Boudicca.

Boudicca was the wife of Prasutagus, king of the Iceni. During Prasutagus' lifetime, the Iceni were a client kingdom to Rome. When Prasutagus died, he did not have a male heir, so he left his wealth to his two daughters and Emperor Nero in the hopes that this show of favor would cause Rome to treat his family well. His hopes were in vain. Tradition says that the Romans not only took Boudicca's land but also raped her daughters. Boudicca had had enough. She raised a rebellious army that included not just the Iceni but other tribes in the area that later became East Anglia (southeast Britain).

Boudicca's rebellion was at first very successful, largely because she struck at a time when the current Roman governor, Suetonius Paulinus, was gone. Boudicca's rebel army burned three cities, Londinium (London), Camulodunum (Colchester), and Verulamium (St. Albans), to the ground and destroyed the Ninth Legion. According to the Romans, the rebellious army also massacred thousands of civilians, although we can't be sure of the numbers because the Roman sources are clearly biased in this situation.

The rebellion was not destined to last, though. Suetonius Paulinus and his army returned from quelling unrest led by the druids in Wales. Boudicca's forces were annihilated, and Boudicca died shortly after. Many believe she poisoned herself after seeing the destruction of her army and the ruin of her rebellion.

Although Boudicca's rebellion was not successful, it demonstrated that there was much unrest with Roman rule. Roman control was still tenuous, but over time its rule became much more firmly established. One of the people most responsible for that was General Agricola.

Agricola and the Expansion of Roman Control

Gnaeus Julius Agricola is most famous for his conquest of the Caledonian tribes. Caledonia was a name used by the Romans to describe the area north of their control, a territory corresponding roughly to modern-day Scotland.

Beginning in the late 70s CE, Agricola expanded Roman control west and north. He firmly subdued the area that would become modern-day Wales and began pushing farther north than any Roman general before him. He had forts and roads built, providing the Romans with important infrastructure to help them maintain control of the territory they conquered.

The northern tribes did not take this Roman expansion lying down. The tribes in the Caledonia territory united under the leadership of Calgacus and faced off against Agricola's forces at the battle of Mons Graupius in 83 CE. We aren't entirely sure where this battle took place, but it was somewhere in northeast Scotland and was a resounding success for Agricola's forces.

Agricola not only conquered the north but also implemented policies designed to Romanize the inhabitants of Britain. These policies included the building of temples, Roman public buildings, and Roman-style houses. The goal was to make the Britons culturally Roman, which would more effectively fold them into the empire and lessen British resistance to Roman rule. Thanks to Agricola, by the end of the 80s CE, Rome's control over Britain was much firmer. Agricola's efforts to bring Roman culture to the Britons had improved Roman control in the south, and his military prowess had allowed the Romans to conquer the north. For the first and only time, Rome had control over most of the island. This control, however, was destined to be short-lived.

The Retreat of Rome and Hadrian's Wall

Shortly after Agricola conquered Scotland, the Romans left this hard-won land. Threats in other parts of the empire forced the emperor to remove legions from Britain. With less personnel, the Romans simply could not hold all the land Agricola had conquered. This began a gradual southward retreat for the Romans. The north had essentially been abandoned, but the Romans stationed there continued to be harassed by local tribes. The border between Roman-controlled territory and the area controlled by the Caledonian tribes (or Picts, as they are also known) continued to move south and was a constant source of skirmishes and conflict.

In 122 CE, the current emperor, Hadrian, decided to personally address the British situation. After traveling to Britain and assessing the situation with his own eyes, Hadrian ordered a wall to be built along the border between Roman-controlled Britain and the wild north.

Hadrian's Wall, as it was aptly named, stretched for seventy-three miles. Spaced along the wall periodically were towers, small forts called fortlets, and forts. There was also a large ditch, called the vallum, dug behind the wall and the forts.

Hadrian's Wall West of Housesteads.
https://commons.wikimedia.org/wiki/File:Hadrian%27s_Wall_west_of_Housesteads_4.jpg

Although this description certainly makes Hadrian's Wall sound like a defensive fortification, it acted more like a border. The towers and forts along the wall were far too spaced out to form a unified front against any invasion. Besides, the Romans manning the walls were trained to meet their opponents in the open rather than defend from the top of a wall. What good was the wall, then? Hadrian's Wall was essentially a buffer. Its physical presence alone was enough to hold off minor threats from the northern tribes, and it also restricted travel, allowing the Romans to better control the border.

Despite taking six years to complete, Hadrian's wall was outdated soon after its completion. Hadrian's successor as emperor, Antoninus Pius, decided to try to extend Roman control northward once again. The result was the Antonine Wall. At thirty-seven miles, it stretched across a narrower part of the island farther north than Hadrian's Wall.

The Antonine Wall, however, did not last. The territory between Hadrian's Wall and the Antonine Wall proved too difficult for the Romans to hold. The Antonine Wall was abandoned, and Hadrian's Wall remained the northern border of Roman-controlled Britain until the end of the Roman occupation. Rome had given up on the north.

Romanization

Rome's efforts to conquer the area that would become Scotland were effectively over well before 200 CE. In the south, however, Roman rule would continue until about 410 CE. Such a long period of occupation was bound to leave its mark on the Britons.

Romanization had begun before the conquest in 43 CE. There was contact between the British Isles and the continent after Julius Caesar's invasion in 54 BCE. Trade took place between Rome and the British tribes, especially the tribes in southeast Britain. Romanization after the conquest began largely with towns. There were two types of Roman settlements in Britain: the *colonia* and the *municipium*. *Coloniae* were settlements founded and populated by Romans. In Britain, the Romans living in *coloniae* were typically ex-legionaries who were given land as payment upon retiring from their legion. Several of Britain's modern cities, such as Colchester, got their start this way.

So, *coloniae* were Roman from the start, but *municipia* were native settlements that were Romanized enough to be recognized by the Roman government as towns. St. Albans is an example of one such town. Despite being originally a British city, St. Albans was burned to the ground during Boudicca's rebellion, indicating that by 60 or 61 CE, it was considered Roman.

The establishment of both *coloniae* and *municipia* was the core of the process of Romanization. Each town managed its own affairs as well as those of the surrounding territory. Thus, when towns became Roman, their influence spread Romanization throughout the countryside.

But how exactly were the towns Roman? In layout, British towns of this era began to resemble their Roman counterparts on the continent. The streets crossed at perpendicular angles, dividing the towns into neat blocks. At the center of each town was the forum, which was a market and gathering place, and the basilica, a building used for public affairs.

Architecturally, the buildings within this Roman design did not resemble what one would find in Italy. Whether as a matter of style or practicality, the architecture of Rome did not catch on in Britain to a large extent. However, if one were to enter these British homes, one would quickly find Roman influence. Features like hypocausts (spaces below a floor used for heating) and mosaics were Roman inventions common in British homes. Archeology has also found further evidence of Romanization in British towns by the Roman coins, pottery, and decorative objects discovered.

Roman coins from the Hoxne Hoard.
https://commons.wikimedia.org/wiki/File:Hoxne_Hoard_coins_5.JPG

Romanization did not stop at the towns, however. Wealthy tribesmen soon began copying Roman influences in country life, as well. Villas (country estates) were built with Roman features. Over time, Latin spread as a common language, and the Britons embraced Roman entertainment and comforts, like amphitheaters and public baths, and even Roman fashions like the toga.

All this created a Britain that was a Roman territory rather than a conquered land. At some point, the people began to consider themselves Romans who lived in Britain rather than Britons.

That is not to say that Britain became a mini-Rome. While the Britons embraced many aspects of Roman life, Britain never achieved the pure scale of Rome. The towns were not as large, and the villas were not as grand as they were in Italy. Once the Romans left, little of Britain's Roman era survived. There were no grand Roman structures like the Colosseum that would stand for the next several hundred years. Britain's prehistoric monuments like Stonehenge proved to be more lasting than its Roman constructions.

Another aspect of Roman life that did not take hold in Britain was religion. Shrines to native gods remained throughout the Roman period, indicating the high persistence of the Briton religious beliefs. While Rome could not replace the native religion, it nevertheless had an impact. Celtic gods were given Roman form, the most famous example being the Celtic goddess of springs, Sulis, who at Bath was combined with the Roman goddess Minerva.

The Roman pantheon may not have replaced the native gods of the Britons, but the Romans introduced another religion that would prove to have an enormous impact on Britain: Christianity. How exactly Christianity came to the shores of Britain remains a topic of legend and debate, but we know for sure that by 314 CE, Britain had at least three Christian bishops who attended the Council of Arles. Christianity would have an immense impact on the Anglo-Saxons and the nation of England, making its introduction to the island in the Roman era one of the most impactful and lasting effects of the Roman occupation.

For more than three centuries, Britain was a Roman province, and this time transformed the culture and people of the island. By 400 CE, the Britons were speaking Latin, living in Roman towns, governing with Roman systems, and using Roman goods. If Britain was so thoroughly

Romanized, what was going to happen when the Romans left?

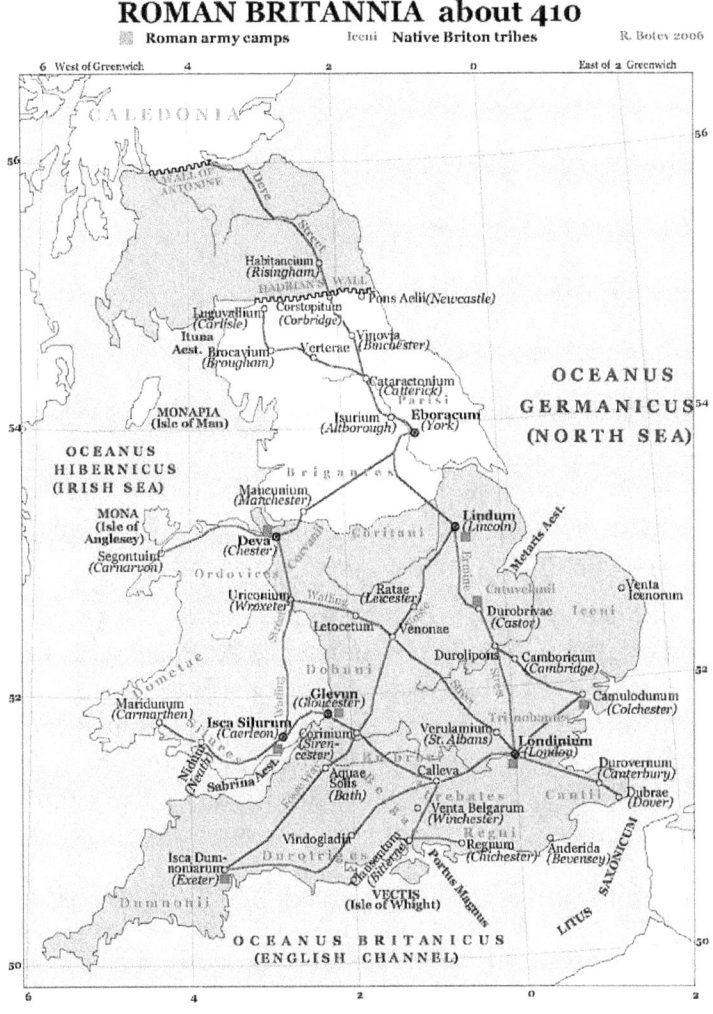

Map of Roman Britain 410.
https://commons.wikimedia.org/wiki/File:Roman_Britain_410_provinces.jpg

Chapter 4: The Anglo-Saxons

History is often repetitive, and one historical drama that has been played out repeatedly in human history is the fall of empires. Rome, for all its might, was no exception to this trope.

By the fifth century, the Roman Empire was collapsing due to a combination of external threats and infighting. As things went from bad to worse, the remote island province of Britannia was far down the list of priorities for Rome. Around 410 CE, the Roman legions were removed from Britain to deal with threats on the continent, and the legions never returned. Britain did not break out of Roman rule; it was thrown to the side by the Romans.

Having a conquering empire set you free with no bloodshed might sound great, but, as we discussed in the last chapter, the Celtic Britons had become rather Romanized. What's more, being a Roman province came with a crucial benefit—Roman legions. Without the legions to protect them, the Celtic Britons were left to defend themselves against all sorts of invaders.

Three main groups took advantage of a Britain without Roman legions: the Picts of Scotland, the Scotti of Ireland, and the Anglo-Saxons from the continent. Eventually, the Anglo-Saxons moved past raiding to settling until the land of Britain became England, the land of the Angles.

The Arrival of the Anglo-Saxons

With the arrival of the Anglo-Saxons, we are finally getting to the English part of English history. But who exactly were the Anglo-Saxons? According to early sources, the Anglo-Saxons were a group consisting of three different tribes of settlers from the continent: the Angles, the Saxons, and the Jutes. The Angles and Saxons were Germanic tribes, and the Jutes were a Norse tribe. These tribes came from northern Europe and settled in southeastern and southern Britain in the fifth and sixth centuries.

We do not have exact dates for the arrival of the Anglo-Saxons. Like the Celtic tribes, the Anglo-Saxons did not have a written language for some time, and as we discussed earlier, the lack of written records leaves historians with a harder job. We know very little about what happened in Britain from around 400 CE, when the Romans departed, to around 600 CE. By this time, seven Anglo-Saxon kingdoms (known as the Heptarchy) had emerged.

This means that the sources we have about the Anglo-Saxon settlement were written long after the events. These traditional sources, such as the Venerable Bede's *Ecclesiastical History of the English People* written in the eighth century, say that the Anglo-Saxons conquered southern Britain in a reign of terror between 400 and 600, annihilating the Celtic tribes and forcing the survivors to flee to what would become the Celtic nations of Wales, Cornwall, and Brittany.

While it is certain the Anglo-Saxons were not nice to the Celtic Britons (they stole their land), it is less certain whether the Anglo-Saxons committed genocide on the scale we originally thought. Another more likely possibility is forced assimilation. The Anglo-Saxons looked down on the Celtic Britons, forcing them into the lowest tier of society as they conquered their land. As a result, the Celtic Britons likely merged into Anglo-Saxon society to avoid social isolation and discrimination.

So, through a mixture of forced migration, assimilation, and murder, the Celtic Britons were replaced by these invaders from northern Europe. By the seventh century, the Anglo-Saxons had consolidated into seven main kingdoms: Mercia, Northumberland, Wessex, Essex, Kent, Sussex, and East Anglia.

Anglo-Saxon Culture

The Anglo-Saxons were here to stay, but what were they like? Writing did not come to the Anglo-Saxons until their conversion to Christianity, so we have no written records of the early Anglo-Saxon period. Later, after writing was introduced, there was still relatively little reliable information about these people. Many of the writings from the time have clear biases and inaccuracies that make them difficult to take completely at face value. This lack of information has caused the Anglo-Saxon period in English history to be known as the Dark Ages, but this is a misleading name based on a biased view.

The term "Dark Ages" is meant to describe a regression of human civilization. A dark age is a time of ignorance and barbarity. But assigning the name Dark Ages to the Anglo-Saxon period has far more to do with the Romans than the Anglo-Saxons. During the Renaissance, the period immediately following the Middle Ages, society saw a renewed interest and veneration for classical Greek and Roman culture. Rome was seen as the birthplace of Western civilization. With such a high view of Rome, it was only natural to assume that their departure from the island of Britain would set its society back. The fact that there were no written historical records to contradict this view did not help matters. The Anglo-Saxons were viewed as a brutish people by historians for a long time.

However, as research on this era has continued and we have learned more about the Anglo-Saxons, we now know that such a view is not only biased but also not true. As with Britain's prehistory, archeology has taught us much of what we know about the Anglo-Saxons. Burial sites like Sutton Hoo show that the Anglo-Saxons had a rich and sophisticated culture. They buried some of their dead with many grave goods, indicating both a social hierarchy and a large amount of wealth. Subsistence farmers barely scraping by could not afford to bury their dead with gold, jewelry, weapons, and more.

Helmet from Sutton Hoo Burial site.
https://commons.wikimedia.org/wiki/File:Sutton.hoo.helmet.jpg

Therefore, we now know that the Anglo-Saxons were a successful and complex society. That being said, Anglo-Saxon life could also be brutal. Anglo-Saxons lived in tribal societies that placed great emphasis on kinship and honor. These values translated into a culture where killing to avenge family members was quite common. The Anglo-Saxons developed *wergild,* a system that set a price on a person's life so that monetary compensation could be made for murder. This was necessary to stop the endless cycle of murders caused by a society that demanded honor and revenge.

Warfare was also a common part of Anglo-Saxon life. Remember that the Anglo-Saxons were technically invaders from the continent. To establish their kingdoms, they had to seize land from the Celtic Britons. Tradition says that the Celtic forces that resisted the Anglo-Saxon invasions were led by the legendary King Arthur, although we don't have any evidence that such a person existed. Regardless, the Anglo-Saxons certainly used military might to seize control of the island, and even after they had gained control, warfare continued.

By the seventh century, seven major Anglo-Saxon kingdoms shared the southeastern region of a small island. There were also Welsh kingdoms to the west and Scottish kingdoms to the north. With so many competing groups crammed into a small geographical area, competition for resources like land often became violent. Warfare was also tempting simply because it led to great gains. Stronger kingdoms could demand tribute from their weaker neighbors, people captured in conflicts could be used or sold as slaves, and treasure and resources could be seized from defeated opponents. In the Anglo-Saxon world, warfare was economics.

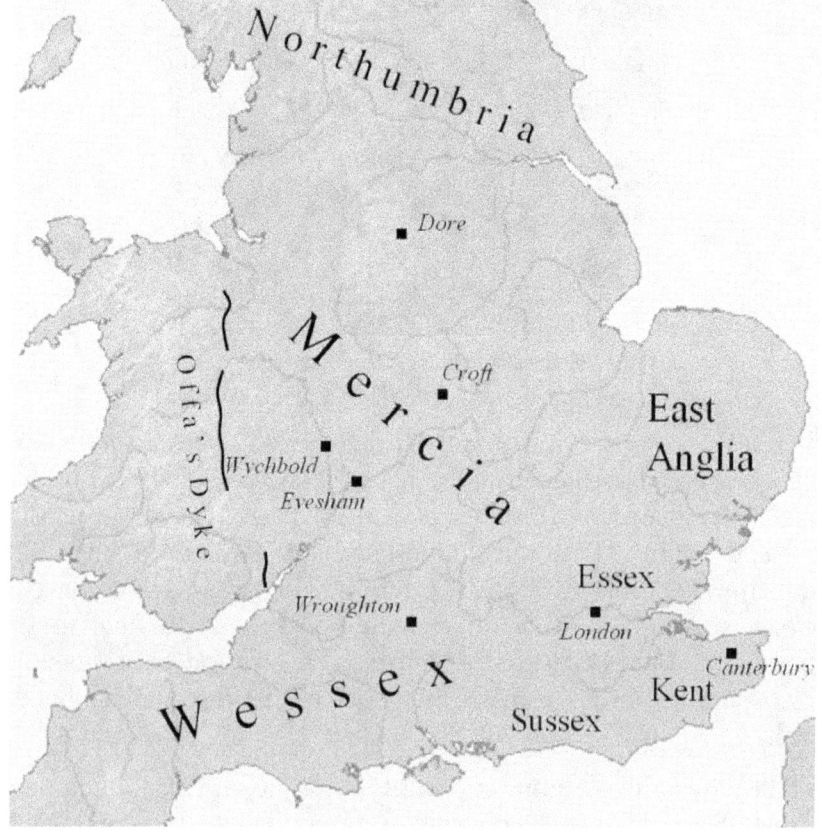

Map of the Anglo-Saxon kingdoms.
https://commons.wikimedia.org/wiki/File:Wiglaf_locations_incl._Offa%27s_Dyke.gif

That doesn't mean the Anglo-Saxons spent all their time fighting. This was still the era of human history where, if human society was to survive, most people needed to be farmers. So, daily life for most Anglo-Saxons would have involved working the land.

Life wasn't all working and fighting for the Anglo-Saxons, though. They also had entertainment. For instance, poetry was a large part of Anglo-Saxon culture. Because of its rhythm, poetry is easier to memorize and listen to, making it excellent entertainment for people without television or easy access to books.

The most famous Anglo-Saxon poem is the epic, *Beowulf*, which follows the titular hero through his adventures slaying monsters. Other examples of Anglo-Saxon poetry include *Caedmon's Hymn, The Seafarer,* and *The Battle of Maldon.*

These poems tell us a lot about what Anglo-Saxon culture valued. Poems like *Beowulf* and *The Battle of Maldon* both tell the tales of heroes who ultimately fall in battle. This tells us that the Anglo-Saxons viewed warfare as more than economic gain. There was a perceived honor in being a warrior and falling in battle. On the other hand, the Anglo-Saxons also wrote poems like *Caedmon's Hymn* and *The Seafarer. Caedmon's Hymn* is, as the name implies, a hymn praising God. *The Seafarer* is from a genre called wisdom poetry that describes the ups and downs of life. *The Seafarer* tells the tale of an exile at sea who must wait for the glory of heaven to find his redemption.

As you can tell from these last two poems, Christian values were a part of Anglo-Saxon culture. The Anglo-Saxons' conversion to Christianity is a key factor in understanding who they were and how they impacted England.

Conversion to Christianity

Christianity brought writing to the Anglo-Saxons and allowed the Anglo-Saxon kingdoms to claim a place in the grand scheme of European politics. Christian tradition says that Joseph of Arimathea, whose tomb Jesus was laid in after his crucifixion, brought Christianity to Britain during the time of the Romans, but there is no historical evidence to support this claim. A later legend says that Pope Gregory I sent Augustine in 597 to convert the Anglo-Saxons after remarking on the beauty of Angle boys in the slave market at Rome. While Augustine may have acted as a missionary to the English, we can hardly give him sole credit for bringing Christianity to England, as it was already on the island in the Roman age.

Irish missionaries likely also played an important role in converting the Anglo-Saxons.

However it arrived, Christianity spread gradually over the island and had a huge influence on the Anglo-Saxons. It changed their holidays, rituals, and even their values. The church would soon be involved in a person's life from birth to marriage to death.

For an entire society to change its religious convictions, the ruling class must change, as well. As we will see much later in English history, it is very difficult to maintain a functioning government system when a ruler and the people are of different religions. Part of the reason Christianity took such a hold on the Anglo-Saxons may therefore be because their rulers were converted.

Many Anglo-Saxon kings converted to Christianity because of the benefits it offered them. One of these benefits sounds relatively simple but has far-reaching implications, and that is writing. Christian monks and missionaries were a literate group in a largely illiterate time. Their ability to write allowed the Anglo-Saxon kings they served to make laws and send orders across larger areas. Writing made the transmission of information far easier and more accurate, letting kings effectively rule much larger areas.

There were many other benefits that the rulers of Anglo-Saxon society gained from Christianity. Rituals like assigning godparents let rulers easily connect themselves with other ruling families. The church and other religious institutions like monasteries also gave rulers another place to appoint people loyal to themselves. Having bishops and monks loyal to the king scattered throughout a kingdom was another way that Christianity helped Anglo-Saxon kings consolidate and grow their power.

To understand why Christianity could offer Anglo-Saxon kings so much power, we need to consider that, previously, there were few public institutions involved in a person's daily life. Anglo-Saxons were concerned with their kin, but beyond the ties of blood, there was little connecting them to their neighbors or rulers. Christianity brought a uniform institution to the Anglo-Saxons. With Christianity, everyone across a kingdom was worshiping at the same time and in the same way. Churches also became important community centers for events like baptisms, marriages, and burials. Monasteries began to function as centers of charity in communities. Thus, Christianity provided institutions that united the

Anglo-Saxons more firmly. The more firmly the people were united, the easier it was for the ruling class to expand its power.

However, it was ultimately not Christianity but something else entirely that at last united the seven Anglo-Saxon kingdoms into a single kingdom known as England.

Chapter 5: The Viking Raids and the Formation of England

In the last chapter, we talked about the Anglo-Saxons, but discussing the people who had settled in the area that would eventually become England as though they were one group can be misleading. The term Anglo-Saxons did not exist at the time. In the seventh and eighth centuries, the people living in England, although they did share many cultural similarities, would not have thought of themselves as one people group.

The seven kingdoms of the Anglo-Saxons were constantly vying for power. At times, one kingdom (particularly Northumbria, Mercia, and Wessex) emerged as the most powerful and required tribute from the others, but there was no consolidation or unity between the kingdoms. It would take a significant external threat to turn the Anglo-Saxon kingdoms into England.

Enter the Vikings

At the very end of the eighth century, the British Isles faced a new threat. Invaders from Scandinavia, known collectively as Vikings, began raiding. The earliest raids date to the 790s but only increased over the next hundred years, and it's not hard to see why. A growing population in Scandinavia was looking for resources, and Britain was a prime target. The now-Christian Anglo-Saxons had built many monasteries furnished with much wealth and inhabited by monks and nuns who would not fight back.

They were easy and profitable targets for the Vikings, who held no religious qualms that would keep them from preying on these religious centers.

You can imagine how much (or rather, how little) resistance a group of armed Viking warriors met with from monks. There was nothing to discourage the raids from continuing, and the fact that many of the monks persistently rebuilt after each devastating raid only meant that the Vikings never seemed to run out of targets.

Of course, the great devastation caused by the Vikings was not simply because they picked easy targets. Even when attacking settlements with inhabitants who fought back, the Vikings were a deadly force. Their longboats were narrow and had shallow draughts, which allowed them to land directly on the beach near settlements. The Vikings could strike quickly before a village knew what was upon them and then be back out to sea again before the victims knew what had happened.

As devastating as these raids were, especially for those living on the coast, we probably wouldn't be discussing them here if the Vikings had stopped at raiding. There must've been something appealing about the British Isles because the Viking raiders turned into something far scarier: Viking settlers.

Much like the Anglo-Saxons before them, around the middle of the ninth century, the Vikings began extending their time in England beyond the raiding season. They started to overwinter (spend the season when the seas were too rough for travel) on the isles, establishing settlements. With the establishment of settlements came larger conflicts with the Anglo-Saxons. Now it was not only coastal towns that had to fear the invaders.

In 865 CE, things went from bad to worse for the Anglo-Saxons. A large army of Vikings landed and soon began to conquer the Anglo-Saxon kingdoms. This huge force was aptly known as The Great Heathen Army. The name, which we get from the Anglo-Saxon Chronicle, reveals a bias toward the invaders, so some historians refer to this force simply as the Great Army or Great Viking Army instead. All three names refer to the same group.

Regardless of what you call it, the Great Army was undoubtedly effective. The Vikings conquered East Anglia, Mercia, and Northumbria with little trouble. Their influence and increasing power in Britain went relatively unchecked for the next decade.

Alfred the Great and the Rise of Wessex

After the initial success of the Great Army's invasion, the Vikings, having conquered three kingdoms with relative ease, had one last major Anglo-Saxon territory to defy them: Wessex.

Wessex had faced Viking onslaughts during the early years after the landing of the Great Army. Their king was even killed in the fighting in 871 CE, leaving his brother Alfred, who was the fifth of five sons, as the new king of Wessex. For a while, there was a reprieve in the fighting, but in 876 CE, the Vikings renewed their efforts to conquer Wessex. In 878 CE, the Vikings looked very close to victory. Their surprise attack on the Wessex fortress at Chippenham forced King Alfred to flee into the marshes of Somerset with only a few of his men. Wessex was all but conquered.

Letting King Alfred escape turned out to be a big mistake. While hiding in the marshes, Alfred and his men conducted a type of guerrilla warfare against the Vikings. Perhaps more importantly, though, Alfred was also able to rebuild his forces. With his new army, Alfred marched against the Vikings later that year. The clash between the two forces took place at Edington, outside the fortress of Chippenham, which the Vikings had occupied after forcing Alfred to flee.

Alfred's forces beat the Vikings, led by Jarl Guthrum, at Edington, forcing the Vikings to flee back to Chippenham, where they surrendered to Alfred after a short siege. The terms of the treaty that followed were relatively simple: Guthrum must be baptized as a Christian, and the Vikings must leave Wessex.

Let's dive into both aspects further because they tell us much about this time and what comes after in English history. First, why would Alfred require Guthrum to be baptized?

In our modern world, it is hard for us to truly grasp how embedded religion was in every aspect of life in the Middle Ages. In fact, there are two mistakes we can make when thinking about religion in this day. One would be to assume that no one took their religion seriously. Religion, Christianity especially, was a huge part of medieval life because so many people believed. It would also be a mistake to think that religion never became a tool of politics or power. When an institution or belief system is so widespread that it melds into every aspect of life, people will try to use it to their own ends.

With these two things in mind, we can perhaps better understand why Alfred would require Guthrum to be baptized, which was a clear sign of conversion to Christianity. To undergo baptism was a sign of political allegiance and a serious commitment. This does not mean that Guthrum necessarily had a change of heart and truly converted religions but that he was at least committed to a public show of peace and, on some level, submission to Alfred. It was not an act that could be conveniently forgotten later. As a religious act, it was a more effective way of binding the peace agreement than a simple shaking of hands.

When we consider the other part of the peace agreement between Alfred and Guthrum, the baptism requirement only makes more sense. Alfred wanted the invading Vikings to leave Wessex, and he did not want them to return. The Vikings had been trying to conquer Wessex for around a decade, and a more permanent treaty was required for a more permanent peace.

For Alfred, achieving that peace meant letting the Vikings have what they had already conquered. Alfred and Guthrum agreed to divide southeastern Britain. Alfred maintained control of Wessex and the smaller Anglo-Saxon kingdoms it dominated (including Kent), and Guthrum and his followers were given the area of East Anglia and parts of Mercia and Northumbria. To agree to let pagans have land conquered by Christians would have been a very unsavory, if prudent, decision, but by having Guthrum baptized, Alfred was in effect negotiating with a fellow Christian ruler.

The area settled by Guthrum and his Vikings became known as the Danelaw because it was under a Danish-style legal system. Since you may be confused at this point, let's take a quick moment to clarify some things. Although we refer to the great invading force that conquered the Anglo-Saxon kingdoms and fought with Alfred as the Vikings, Alfred and his contemporaries referred to these people as the Danes. That's because the Vikings that invaded southern Britain were Danes. However, for the sake of correctness, we should also point out that not all Vikings are Danish. The Viking raiders that attacked other parts of the British Isles such as Ireland and Scotland were Norse. "Vikings" is a general term that refers to the raiders from the Scandinavian countries of this period.

Thanks to the Vikings, Wessex was now the dominant Anglo-Saxon kingdom on the island, and Alfred was the premier ruler, but England still did not exist. The Vikings still controlled huge chunks of what had been Anglo-Saxon land.

Lasting Peace?

If the peace arrangement created by Guthrum and Alfred had lasted, England might not have been formed. However, based on what happened next, we can assume neither party took the peace established after the battle of Edington seriously despite the baptism and setting of boundaries.

By 885 CE, seven years after the Battle of Edington, Alfred was again repelling Danes/Vikings from Kent. This invasion was supported by the Danes of East Anglia (Guthrum's people) and was a breach of the peace that had been established. Still, Alfred was not simply a victim of Viking war lust. The following year, Alfred captured London, an important strategic position between the Anglo-Saxon-controlled area and the land controlled by the Danes.

England at the time of the Danelaw.
https://commons.wikimedia.org/wiki/File:Britain_886.jpg

According to John Asser, a contemporary biographer who knew Alfred personally, this act of retaking London earned Alfred the acceptance of the other Anglo-Saxons as their king. However, we do not consider this the start of the Kingdom of England, for much of Anglo-Saxon territory remained under Danish rule.

With the possession of London, Alfred may have intended to launch new assaults to drive the Danes from the island, but he never got the chance. He was forced to go on the defensive again in 892 CE against Danish forces from the continent. By the time he died in 899 CE, Alfred had made no more progress toward retaking the rest of the Anglo-Saxon kingdoms. That was a task left up to Alfred's children.

But before we move on to Alfred's children, we should spend more time talking about Alfred because he is one of the few kings in history to have received the moniker "the Great."

Alfred the Great from the Brief Abridgement of the Chronicles of England.
https://commons.wikimedia.org/wiki/File:Alfred_the_Great_in_the_Brief_Abridgement_of_the_Chronicles_of_England.jpg

As he is better known to history, Alfred the Great did far more than save the Anglo-Saxons from the Vikings. He was also a scholar and skilled administrator. Alfred worked to improve literacy rates in his kingdom and translated several prominent works into English to make their knowledge available to those who did not know Latin. He translated several works himself and had others translated in his name. This promotion of the English language also helped create a greater sense of a single English identity.

As a ruler, Alfred was judicious. He was responsible for the creation of a law code that gave the Anglo-Saxons, who previously had many different laws and legal systems, a more united legal structure. While this might seem like a boring fact, the establishment of a single law code is vastly important. There could be no unified kingdom and thus no England without a single legal system. A king could not effectively rule an area with a dozen different sets of laws. Thus, although Alfred himself did not unite the Anglo-Saxons into the nation we now know as England, the work he did in stopping the advance of the Danes and beginning to unify the Anglo-Saxons made the formation of England possible.

The Start of England

If Alfred the Great did not form England, who was the first king of England? It took the military and diplomatic work of Alfred's son and grandson to put the Danelaw back under Anglo-Saxon control. In 927, Alfred's grandson Athelstan became the first king to effectively rule all the Anglo-Saxon lands. This, however, was not the beginning of a long line of English kings passing the throne from father to son. While that might be how a monarchy ideally functions, in the tumultuous Middle Ages, it rarely went that smoothly. When Athelstan died in 939, he did not have a son, so the throne went to his half-brother, Edmund I.

Then, shockingly, the Vikings invaded again. This time, it was Norse Vikings (not the Danes) based in Dublin who attacked and seized control of Northumbria and raided the Midlands. Just like that, the unification of Anglo-Saxons that Athelstan had achieved was over.

But this situation also did not last long. By 944, Edmund I had regained control of the Midlands and Northumbria. A united Anglo-Saxon kingdom was restored, but things still weren't over. When Edmund I was killed by an outlaw in 949, his brother Eadred took the throne, as

Edmund's children were still too young to rule. Eadred's reign witnessed rebellion from Northumbria, but he had firmly consolidated his control over the region before he died in 955. His successor was his nephew, Eadwig, who became king at just fifteen years old.

Eadwig was not a popular king. His poor handling of the church and other powerful members in his court led to both Mercia and Northumbria pledging their allegiance to his fourteen-year-old younger brother, Edgar, in 957. Eadwig's support was so low that this arrangement was accepted, and the kingdom was effectively split, with Edgar ruling Mercia and Northumbria and Eadwig ruling Wessex and Kent. Once again, the unity of the Anglo-Saxons had been destroyed.

This, too, only lasted a short while. King Eadwig died two years later in 959, and Edgar became the sole ruler of the Anglo-Saxons. With his reign, England began to see a more stable existence as a single kingdom. Edgar was the first king to officially be crowned in a coronation ceremony as the King of England. His coronation took place late in his reign in 973 as a celebration of the stability England had experienced under him. It was not until later that coronations began to take place at the beginning of the monarch's rule.

Stained glass window depicting King Edgar at All Souls Chapel.
https://commons.wikimedia.org/wiki/File:King_Edgar_from_All_Souls_College_Chapel.png

A United Kingdom

Thus, thanks largely to the Vikings, England came into existence. The external threat the Vikings presented forced England to unify in a way that nothing else could. And, although it had a bit of a rocky start, the unification of the English that Alfred the Great started was well established by the time of Edgar's coronation in 973. Over the next century, this sense of collective identity grew stronger as the Wessex dynasty continued to rule. Common language, common laws, a common king, and even common local administration all worked together to create a common people. However, England would not always remain exclusively the land of the English. In 1066, another group arrived and brought some big changes.

Chapter 6: The Norman Conquest

The Wessex dynasty included the first kings of England, but they were not destined to rule the country forever. Keeping the throne in a single dynasty is a lot harder than you might think. Two major issues stop dynasties from continuing. One is a lack of heirs. If a family can't produce the next generation, it will ultimately lose the throne. The other problem that can interrupt a dynasty is a hostile takeover. To a certain degree, it took might to keep a throne in the Middle Ages.

In 1066, one of the most famous years in English history, England found itself facing both problems simultaneously. Their king had died without an heir, and not one but several invaders landed in the hopes of seizing the throne and the kingdom by force. This is the story of the Norman Conquest.

Background

With an interruption from 1016-1042 when England was again invaded and temporarily ruled by the Danes, the Wessex dynasty ruled from the time of Athelstan to Edward the Confessor.

Edward the Confessor ruled from 1042 to 1066, directly following the Danish interruption. He was called "the Confessor" for his piety, which included a supposed vow to celibacy that extended even into his marriage. Whether or not Edward was celibate remains a point of contention, but regardless, when he died in 1066, he did not have any heirs. He therefore named his most powerful advisor as his heir: Harold Godwinson.

Harold would have to fight, however, if he wanted to keep the throne. The death of a childless king was just too much of an opportunity for many. The first threat Harold faced was not the Normans, though. Harold's brother, Tostig, and the King of Norway, Harald Hardrada, joined forces and attacked York. Harold hurried north to meet them.

Harold's first attempt to beat off rival claimants to the throne was a resounding success. At the Battle of Stamford Bridge on September 25, 1066, Harold's forces were victorious, and both of his rivals were killed in the fighting. Harold had proven he could defend his right to the throne, but he wasn't done. There was another person who felt he had a claim to the English throne: William of Normandy.

Now why in the world would the Duke of Normandy think he had a right to the English crown? In short, William claimed that Edward had named him as his successor and, what's more, that Harold Godwinson had promised to support William's claim. How much truth there is to William's claims remains debatable. Edward indeed had ties to Normandy due to his time spent in exile there. Edward even caused tension as king when he began appointing too many Normans to positions in his government. It is therefore not impossible that Edward would name William as his successor.

The other part about Harold promising to honor William's claim seems less likely. It was a rather convenient excuse for William because it gave him justification with the pope for invading England to push his claim. Such a claim may even have been forced from Harold during a diplomatic mission gone wrong a few years prior, but it is highly doubtful that Harold felt such an oath binding. Regardless of whether Harold had sworn an oath or not, he was not going to hand the throne over to William without a fight. William thus gathered an army and sailed across the channel.

The Battle of Hastings

On September 28, only three days after the Battle of Stamford Bridge and while Harold and his forces were still far in the north, William and his men landed in southern England. Instead of marching inland from this point, William made Hastings his base and waited for Harold to come to him, burning the surrounding countryside to entice Harold to come to the rescue.

And Harold did exactly that, rushing his army southward to face the Norman forces. Although we cannot be sure of Harold's reasons for rushing to engage William, there can be no doubt it was a military blunder. By trying to move his forces so quickly, Harold lost parts of his army and did not have time to gather any more men before confronting William on October 14, 1066.

Despite these disadvantages, the Battle of Hastings was far from a Norman rout. The English formed a shield wall on top of an incline to withstand the charges from the Norman cavalry. The battle raged for most of the day, with each side unable to break the other. Ultimately, the English forces, which were comprised entirely of foot soldiers, could not break the Normans. The shield wall was a strong defensive formation, but it lacked the offensive surge needed to scatter and destroy the Normans. The Norman cavalry, on the other hand, eventually broke through the shield wall, killing the English leaders—including Harold. Thus ended the brief reign of Harold Godwinson.

Part of the Bayeux Tapestry showing Harold's death.
https://commons.wikimedia.org/wiki/File:Bayeux_Tapestry_scene57_Harold_death.jpg

Having defeated Harold, William made his way slowly toward London. With no one of real power to resist him, the leading men of England accepted the inevitable and submitted to William before he arrived in London. He was crowned king on Christmas Day in Westminster Abbey. The Normans had conquered England.

England under the Conqueror

The Norman Conquest did far more than give England a new king. The new regime implemented quite a few changes. One of the first things a conquering king must worry about is staying in control. To cement his hold on the country, William went on a castle-building spree, erecting the first at Hastings before he had even conquered England. Surprisingly, before 1066, England had relatively few castles. The houses of the elites in Anglo-Saxon England were not built with extreme defense in mind, and the towns were too big to be defended well.

Building a network of castles allowed William to keep a firm grip on his new country. Castles were defensible places from which power could be wielded since they held garrisons that could be used to deal with any rebellions. William's castle-building thus gave him strong footholds all over the country.

Castles were not enough to stop a rebellion, however. In the first five years of his reign, William faced several rebellions as the English chafed at the new rule. A major uprising in the north in 1069 made William so enraged that he commanded his army to raze the area, burning food supplies and causing devastation that lasted for years.

Still, by 1071, William's rule was fairly secure, and there were more changes to come. The Conqueror brought several ideas from the continent that he implemented in England, feudalism being perhaps the most influential.

Although we may think feudalism applies to all the Middle Ages, England before 1066 did not have a feudal system. Feudalism refers to when a tenant is granted land (called a fief) from a lord, swearing allegiance to the lord for the right to work the land. Although people in Anglo-Saxon England swore allegiance to the lords and king, they did not receive their land from lords (they were not tenants), which is the key component of feudalism.

While feudalism as an idea came from the continent, in England, William introduced a feudal system that existed nowhere else. As a conqueror, William felt that all of England belonged to him. He could thus parcel out the land however he saw fit, giving large chunks of the land to his Norman supporters. William even considered land held by the church to be under his control, with bishops and abbots also his tenants.

This meant that all of England was held by the king, and every landowner in England received his land from the king. These "tenants-in-chief" who were granted land directly from the king then parceled out the land to their supporters, who swore similar oaths to them. Thus, the feudal chain was created. Nowhere else in Europe did feudalism exist in such a perfect hierarchy, with the king ultimately owning all the land. This was only made possible by the circumstances of the Norman Conquest.

As the person who owned the land, the king had several important privileges in the feudal system. Everyone who held land had to supply knights for the king's army. Fees must be paid to the king upon the death of the tenant if the land was to pass to the heir. If there was no heir, the land returned to the king, and if the heir was a minor, the land returned to the king until the minor came of age. Meanwhile, they were a ward of the king. As the ultimate landowner, the king also had control over the marriage of widows who controlled land and heiresses set to inherit land.

What all these privileges amount to is a lot of political control. The hand of a wealthy heiress can be quite the political bargaining tool. This system also meant the king had direct control over more land than anyone else, which starkly contrasted with the previous Anglo-Saxon system. By the time of Edward the Confessor, several nobles had more land and wealth than the king. Under feudalism, the king was undoubtedly the most powerful man in the kingdom.

The Normans brought other changes, as well. Because William rewarded his followers with land, most of England soon lay in Norman hands. However, many of these Normans had no interest in moving to England. They simply wanted the wealth that could be gained from their new property. They were far more interested in receiving money than goods from the land. This desire led to a decrease in slavery, as the Normans preferred tenants who paid rather than slaves who produced goods. This doesn't necessarily mean people became freer, though. Under feudalism, a farmer who rented land from a lord could not leave the land and had to pay fees to his lord for actions such as having a daughter marry.

The emphasis on land that the feudal system relied on brought another change to England. In Anglo-Saxon England, a family was a large group that consisted of many extended relatives. Wealth and power came largely from who your family was, and land was often distributed among several relatives upon the death of the landowner, the overall goal being to keep the family strong. However, with the Normans came a narrowing of the sense of family. The Normans used the practice of primogeniture, which is when the entire estate passes intact to the eldest son. Primogeniture kept land together, which allowed the wealthy to consolidate larger holdings. This practice of passing everything to one person resulted in a greater focus on the immediate family and a narrowing of the sense of family duty and responsibility toward extended family. It was a cultural shift that would echo down into the Victorian age.

These changes highlight only some of the major impacts the Norman Conquest had on England. It was an event that shook and changed the kingdom to its core. But if it was such a dramatic change, why is England still English? What ultimately happened to the Normans?

The End of Norman Rule

The end of Norman rule was shockingly similar to the beginning. It all started with a king who did not have an heir. Henry I, the fourth son of William the Conqueror and the third Norman king to rule England, had children. His son William was set to become the next king but died unexpectedly during the sinking of the *White Ship* (an infamous incident in 1120 where a ship carrying many elite members of English society sank in the channel).

The sinking of the *White Ship* left Henry I with only one living child, his daughter Matilda, who had been married to the Holy Roman Emperor and later married the Count of Anjou. Henry I proclaimed his daughter his heir, but his Anglo-Norman court did not like it. When Henry died in 1135, the court put his nephew, Stephen of Blois, on the throne instead, and Matilda was none too happy about it.

Thus began a nearly two-decade-long civil war known as The Anarchy. While the name is a bit dramatic, it gives us a good idea of just how chaotic this time was for England. The war between Stephen and Empress Matilda proved to be largely a stalemate, with neither side gaining a decisive victory to end the war. This created a situation where the country was broken up into smaller units, each ruled by different powerful people, including more than just Stephen and Matilda. Their allies, such as Earl Robert, Empress Matilda's half-brother, ruled over their own sections of England at one point. The Scottish king, David, took advantage of the situation to seize control of land in the north. All these different rulers meant that everything from coins to laws differed throughout the country.

And if that wasn't chaotic enough, there was a complete breakdown of law and order in the borderlands between these competing sections. England had broken into pieces.

Strangely enough, it was not a battle that ended this time in English history but an agreement. Having lost his heir, Stephen agreed to make Empress Matilda's son, Henry, his new heir. All parties were satisfied by this, and in 1153, eighteen years after it had started, The Anarchy ended. Only a year later, Stephen died, and Matilda's son became Henry II, starting a new dynasty.

Although Henry II was the son of Matilda and thus the great-grandson of William the Conqueror, he is not considered a member of the Norman line since lineage was traced through the father during this period. Instead, Henry II's dynasty is known by the last name of his father, Geoffrey Plantagenet.

Chapter 7: The Plantagenets

The Plantagenets ruled England from 1154 to 1485. While previous dynasties that ruled England had struggled due to a lack of legitimate heirs, the Plantagenets did not have that problem. The first Plantagenet king, Henry II, had five sons. The succession was certainly secure, but Henry II would eventually learn that too many heirs could also be a problem.

Henry II

Before getting to Henry II's family problems, though, let's take a moment to understand just who Henry II was. During The Anarchy, the English king had not managed to successfully rule over all of England, but when Henry II took the English throne, the opposite became true: Henry II's realm extended far beyond England. Henry's father was the Count of Anjou, which gave Henry control of the territories of Anjou and Maine upon his father's death. He was granted the title Duke of Normandy by the King of France, and when he married Eleanor of Aquitaine, he became Duke of Aquitaine and Gascony. Thus, when Henry Plantagenet became Henry II in 1154, he had quite the empire.

Map of the Angevin Empire 1190.
*Blank map of Europe.svg: maixderivative work: Alphathon, CC BY-SA 4.0
<https://creativecommons.org/licenses/by-sa/4.0>, via Wikimedia Commons:
https://commons.wikimedia.org/wiki/File:Angevin_Empire_1190.svg*

Now, although Henry Plantagenet was the king of England, the Angevin Empire was not necessarily an English empire. Henry II never consolidated his lands into a single territory. England remained separate from Anjou, Aquitaine, Normandy, etc. They simply had the same ruler. In fact, in his status as a Duke of Normandy, for instance, Henry Plantagenet's overlord was technically the King of France. The impact of the English king having so much land in France would ultimately have quite a few repercussions, but we will examine that more closely in the next chapter.

Henry II had so much land in France that he was the greatest landholder in France (holding more land than the King of France), and he spent most of his time on the continent and not in England. Because of this, Henry II worked to create a more effective administrative and bureaucratic system to run the country in his absence. For instance, his legal reforms established better central authority where judges were appointed by the king, and all justice came from the king's law.

These legal reforms attempted to correct a situation that had arisen under the feudal system started by William the Conqueror. In feudalism, barons were the king's tenants but could exercise similar feudal powers over those under them in the social hierarchy. Just as the king could demand marriage fees and give out land, barons could do these things with their land, as well. They could hold court, appoint officials, and generally make working decisions for all land they controlled.

This created an administrative problem. Because the king was at the top of the feudal chain, he rarely made practical decisions that impacted people directly. It was the barons deciding if someone was guilty or innocent, whether someone could get married, collecting taxes, and doing the other legal and governmental things that kept the country running. However, barons did these things however they saw fit, which made for a lot of different governmental procedures operating side by side. This created a situation where, despite not being at the top of the feudal chain, barons could wield more practical power than the king. The king's power was largely abstract, but the power of the barons was very concrete. By centralizing the legal system, Henry II took legal authority away from the barons and gave it back to the king.

The barons were not the only ones who became targets of Henry II's legal reforms. Inevitably, Henry II came into conflict with the church. At this point, when clerics were accused of a secular crime like rape, murder, theft, etc., they were tried and sentenced in church courts—a situation which almost always resulted in light sentencing, such as fasting or doing penance. Henry II saw this as a miscarriage of justice and, in 1164, created the Constitutions of Clarendon to rectify it. The constitutions simply stated that, while clerics were to be tried in church courts, they would be sentenced in the king's courts. The church did not like Henry II trying to step into their affairs one bit. It was an inevitable clash between church and state, and it led to one of the most infamous events in English history.

One of the most violent protesters to Henry II's Constitutions of Clarendon was the Archbishop of Canterbury, Thomas Becket. Becket had been a friend to Henry II before being appointed archbishop, and it is perhaps for this reason that Henry II did not take his protest well. Becket was forced into exile in France in 1165, spending five years there before finally returning to England in 1170. Upon his return, Becket promptly got the Archbishop of York suspended by the pope and excommunicated two other English bishops for their role in crowning Henry's son as heir (a ritual normally performed by the Archbishop of Canterbury).

As you can imagine, Henry II was not amused, and what happened next is slightly unclear. The story goes that when Henry II received word of Becket's actions toward the other English clergy, he burst out angrily, exclaiming, "Will no one rid me of this troublesome priest!" Four knights who were present took his exclamation seriously and decided to rid the king of this pest. Riding to Canterbury, they accosted Becket, murdering him at the altar.

Thomas Becket is murdered by Reginald Fitzurse, Hugh de Morville, William de Tracy, and Richard le Breton.
https://commons.wikimedia.org/wiki/File:Murder_of_Thomas_Becket.jpg

We do not know if this was Henry II's intention or how involved in the murder he was. However, once the deed was done, it quickly became clear that murdering a priest in a church was not a good look. Becket became a saint and martyr, and Canterbury turned into a pilgrimage site. Henry II even had to travel there to offer penance for his role in the murder, whether intentional or not.

The story of Thomas Becket is illustrative of not only the conflict between church and state but also the character of Henry II. He was an extremely competent administrator with a good head for government, but he did not always handle people effectively, and this would prove problematic, especially with his family.

The Sons of Henry II

Henry II had four adult sons: Henry, Geoffrey, Richard, and John. Henry II attempted to keep his sons happy by dividing his realm among them.

But this strategy only frustrated his sons because, despite their titles, Henry did not allow them any real authority. For instance, he made his oldest son, Henry the Younger, his co-regent, but this amounted to little more than a fancy title.

The brothers also spent a lot of time quarreling over who got what. In 1173, Henry and Richard rebelled against their father for trying to give John more land. Their mother Eleanor supported the rebellion and spent the rest of Henry II's life in house arrest for it. After squashing the rebellion they had started, Henry II forgave his sons, but they had not learned their lesson. In 1181, Richard and Henry came to blows over Aquitaine. In 1183, Henry died, followed three years later by Geoffrey. This left only two sons to squabble, but that was enough. Richard joined forces with Philip II of France to fight against his father, and when John joined sides with his brother, it was all the king could take. Henry II was defeated and died in 1189, with many believing that the rebellion of his sons had hastened his end.

Richard was now king of England, but more attractive to Richard were all the French lands he had also inherited. Richard ruled for about ten years, but he only spent six months in England, preferring his continental holdings or to be on a Crusade. Indeed, Richard I is more often known as Richard the Lionheart for his crusading and military prowess.

Richard I the Lionheart, King of England by Merry-Joseph Blondel.
https://commons.wikimedia.org/wiki/File:Richard_coeur_de_lion.jpg

Considering that he spent less than a year in England, Richard's reputation as a fantastic king is largely undeserved. The popular view of him today has been largely skewed by the story of Robin Hood, which portrays Richard as a beloved and noble king. In reality, Richard seems to have cared little for England or administration. His capture during the Crusades by Muslims and subsequent ransom put a great financial burden on his people, and his military victories in the Crusades did not benefit England. As a king, Richard preferred warfare to law writing, and after a decade of leaving England to rule itself, he died during a siege in France in 1199.

Richard the Lionheart did not have an heir, so his brother John became king after him. Like Richard, the story of Robin Hood, which portrays John as a despicable tyrant, has also influenced how King John is viewed today. However, in John's case, the reality is a lot more complicated.

While his brother was known as "the Lionheart," John ended up with a much less flattering nickname: John Lackland. The nickname came from the fact that John, as the youngest son of Henry II, could not expect to inherit any significant land. This name turned out to be ironic for two reasons. John went on to inherit his father's holdings but then lost them. Thus, the nickname proved true but in an unexpected way.

John's inheritance of all his brother's land was a bit rocky, with Philip II, the King of France, initially recognizing his nephew, Arthur, as the inheritor of Anjou and Maine. However, John made concessions, and a year later had control over all of Richard's lands. The Angevin Empire was intact but not for long.

While we can sometimes be too harsh on King John, it's hard to argue that what happened next was not at least partially his fault. John had his marriage with his first wife dissolved to marry Isabella, the heiress to Angoulême, in 1200. Now, in some ways, this was a politically savvy marriage. It helped John to better secure his land in the south. But what was not politically savvy was failing to make things right with Hugh de Lusignan, the man Isabella had been betrothed to.

Lusignan complained about John to Philip II, which was all the excuse the ambitious French king needed. When John refused to appear before Philip II, war broke out, and King John did not make a good showing. While he had some initial success at the start of the war, his suspicious nature and poor decisions drove away his allies and lost battles. By 1206, he had lost Normandy, Anjou, and Maine. The loss cannot be placed entirely at John's feet. At this point, it would've been very hard for England to beat France even with a more competent leader. England had been strained funding Richard's military campaigns, and the French had more resources.

John was forced back to England, but he only had one goal: recovering the lands he had lost, which required a lot of funding. War is expensive, after all. John used every trick he could think of to gather more money from his people, including exploiting his feudal rights over his barons. This, along with instances of arbitrary justice where King John decided cases based on his whims rather than the law, sowed growing discontent among the barons of England. In 1215, a civil war known as the First Barons' War broke out.

Just like in France, John did not have much military success and soon found himself negotiating with the barons. On June 19, 1215, King John signed the Magna Carta, a document protecting the rights of the barons against the king and insisting that the king had to uphold the common law. The document is often seen as an important milestone in the protection of human rights.

It is possible to both over and understate the importance of the Magna Carta. It provided protection from tyranny, but only for the barons, not for everyday people. Still, the ideas and language of the Magna Carta found their way into later movements, such as the American and French revolutions of the eighteenth century. The Magna Carta was an important document for what it later came to represent but not for the impact it had at the time. It was overturned by the pope shortly after it was signed, and the civil war continued, ending when John died and his nine-year-old son became Henry III in 1216.

The Rise of Parliament

Henry III ruled from 1216 to 1272. During that time, he, like his more infamous father, also had conflicts with the barons, inciting the Second Barons' War from 1264 to 1267. It was during this conflict that Henry III's son, Edward, began to show a martial prowess that would have drastic consequences for not only England but the entire island of Great Britain.

When Henry III died in 1272, his son became Edward I. Edward the Confessor from centuries earlier was known primarily as the Confessor, so even though Edward I is technically the second English King Edward, he is still known as Edward I. Edward I inherited a throne that was in many ways a mess. The royal coffers were, if not empty, at least severely strained, and after two civil wars, the relationship between the king and the barons was still tense.

Correcting both issues required Edward I to learn how to work with a new institution: Parliament. The earliest idea for Parliament appears to have been the 1215 Magna Carta, which said that barons had the right to advise the king. At this point, this group of advisors was referred to as the Great Council, but eventually, it became known as Parliament. By Edward I's reign, it was clear that Parliament was there to stay. While it did not yet have all the powers it has today, Parliament had one very important right: to approve taxation.

This one power gave Parliament the ear of the king. If the king wanted revenue, he needed taxes, and if he wanted taxes, he needed Parliament's approval, and if he wanted their approval, he had to listen to them. This does not mean Parliament could bully the king. He still had ultimate power, but now there was a platform for grievances and opinions to be aired and an incentive for the king to take them seriously.

Edward I was greatly interested in replenishing the royal finances, especially to wage his wars, which we will discuss in more detail in a moment. Thus, he learned how to work with Parliament, not only enduring it but using Parliament as a tool to govern the realm. It was the start of a different type of kingship. With the rise of Parliament, Edward I's England was gaining a greater national sense of identity. The government was no longer just the king but the bureaucracy that surrounded him, particularly his council, which made up the core of Parliament. This was a transformation from the more feudal style of kingship where all power rested in and came from the king.

Wales and Scotland

With his predecessors having lost most their lands in France, Edward I set out to expand his kingdom, but he aimed closer to home.

Edward I.
Firkin, CC0, via Wikimedia Commons:
https://commons.wikimedia.org/wiki/File:King_Edward_I.png

Edward I conquered Wales with a brutally simple but effective strategy. Invading for the first time in 1277, Edward I fielded an enormous army against which the Welsh stood virtually no chance. Then, after overwhelming them with the initial strike, Edward I built many castles to cement his control—a tactic that William the Conqueror had employed after conquering England back in 1066. Although there were revolts, from this point, Wales was under the control of the English (though it would be a long time before the two nations were officially joined).

Edward I did not stop at Wales, though. He also had plans to conquer Scotland, an ambition which earned him the nickname "Hammer of the Scots." He invaded his northern neighbor in 1296, but he did not have the funds needed to repeat what he had done in Wales. The conquest of Scotland was therefore much slower, and despite stiff resistance from the Scots, it appeared that eventually Edward I would conquer Scotland, too. However, Edward I died in 1307 before the campaign was finished, leaving the conquest of Scotland to his son, Edward II.

Fortunately for Scotland, Edward II was not his father. The Scots, led by Robert the Bruce, defeated the English and Edward II at the Battle of Bannockburn in 1314, securing Scottish independence for the next four hundred years.

Edward II also failed to mimic his father in another way: keeping his barons happy. With a reputation for blatant favoritism and incompetent government, Edward II was not well-liked. He was ultimately deposed by a plot hatched by his wife and her lover, becoming the first English king to be forced off the throne while still alive. His son, Edward III, was put on the throne in his place in 1327 at the age of fourteen.

These were the first six kings of the Plantagenet dynasty and the England they ruled. The kingdom that Edward III took over in 1327 was much smaller than that ruled by Henry II, but it was also a bit more English. By 1327, years of discontented barons had forced the English king to give more consideration to the people he ruled. However, English kings had still not lost all interest in France.

Chapter 8: The Hundred Years' War and the Black Death

The fourteenth century was one of the most turbulent times in English history. Despite various wars, the general population of England had been increasing steadily over the twelfth and thirteenth centuries. But, by the end of the fourteenth century, around a third to a half of the English population was dead.

Not only would the fourteenth century see death on an enormous scale, but there was political turmoil. By the end of the century, England had entered a war that would last over a hundred years and seen its first popular uprising. It was enough to make many people think the world was ending, and in some ways, they were right. By the time the 1300s ended, medieval society was starting to crumble and transform.

So, what exactly happened? Let's back up a bit and start with 1315, the year of the famine.

The Great Famine

As we just noted, until the fourteenth century the English population had been steadily increasing. Agricultural production was improving, and with the ability to feed more mouths, population growth was inevitable. This situation made the entire population of Europe highly susceptible to food shortages, which is exactly what happened in 1315.

Periods of heavy rain and cooler temperatures rotted the crops and made it impossible to even make hay for the livestock. Farmers, unable to get food from their land, sold it and moved to large population centers in the hopes of buying food. But the extreme demand and low supply made prices skyrocket. There simply wasn't enough to go around. Farming conditions did not recover until 1322, and by then, about 15 percent of the English population had died of starvation.

Despite its great devastation, England recovered from The Great Famine relatively quickly. The population and economy were back to normal by 1330. Still, the event impacted all of Europe and left a traumatic memory with all those who survived. Medieval society had been completely unable to handle the crisis caused by the weather, and eventually, changes were made to government structure to better handle such wide-scale events. However, the fourteenth century still had a lot more to throw at England.

The Hundred Years' War

As we discussed in the previous chapter, English kings had held land in France since the time of Henry II. They had lost most of that land during the reign of King John, but the connections between France and England were still there. In 1337, Edward III decided it was time to push those ties, declaring his right to the French throne.

Now, this claim wasn't completely crazy. Edward III and the current French king, Philip the Fair, both shared a great-grandfather who had been king of France. When the direct line of the French monarchy failed, Philip the Fair ended up on the throne, but technically Edward III had just as much of a blood claim to the throne.

Still, becoming king of France was probably not Edward III's plan. What brought France and England to war in 1337 was not the French throne but French land, specifically Aquitaine. France claimed that Aquitaine was a French duchy subject to the French king. England believed that Aquitaine was part of its feudal territory since the time of Henry II. Under the systems of the day, both sides had a point, and Aquitaine was a rich enough holding for both to be prepared to fight over it. Thus, the Hundred Years' War began.

The name of this war in slightly misleading for two reasons. First, it lasted longer than a hundred years, from 1337 to 1453. It was also less an ongoing war and more a series of campaigns with frequent temporary truces and interruptions. France and England were at war for over a hundred years, but they were not actively fighting for a hundred years.

There are too many major battles for us to delve into here. Names like Crecy, Poitiers, Agincourt, Orleans, and Castilian would become forever seared in English memory. Some, like Agincourt, were great victories that would become almost mythic in the English psyche. Others, like Castilian, the last major battle of the war, were crushing defeats. While the English were initially very successful in the war, winning early battles like Crecy, the English had lost all land in France by the end of the war in 1453 (except for Calais, which the French would not recover until 1558).

King Henry V of England at the Battle of Agincourt, France, October 25, 1415. Line engraving, 19th century.
https://commons.wikimedia.org/wiki/File:King_Henry_V_of_England_at_the_Battle_of_Agincourt,_1415.jpg

War against France was ultimately an extremely costly endeavor that gained England very little. It caused periods of severe taxation on the English people, resulting in a popular uprising. The constant campaigning also created a nobility with high levels of military drive and know-how, which would prove disastrous during the internal conflicts of the fifteenth century, which we will discuss in the following chapter. Finally, a hundred years of war utterly destroyed relations between the two countries. England and France would remain fierce rivals until World War I. But not even the outbreak of this conflict was the most disruptive event of the fourteenth century.

The Black Death

In 1347, the Black Death struck Europe, and nothing would ever be the same. But before we get into precisely what happened, what exactly is the Black Death? The Black Death refers to the specific outbreak of plague that hit Europe from 1347 to 1351. "Plague" in this sense does not refer to the outbreak of any disease. It is a term that refers to a specific disease caused by the bacterium *Yersinia pestis*. Plague still exists today, but thanks to antibiotics, it is no longer the threat it was in 1347.

The Black Death was also not the first time that plague had affected human populations. There had been outbreaks before, but nothing of the scale and devastation of the Black Death. Estimates state that the disease killed between a third and a half of the entire population of Europe (the disease also spread to Asia and Africa, where it caused similar levels of devastation). Entire villages were wiped out.

To put it in perspective, the second deadliest pandemic in history was the outbreak of Spanish influenza in 1918, which killed 3 percent of the world's population. The Black Death killed around 50 percent of people in Africa, Asia, and Europe. Almost no other event in history comes close to that level of destruction. How then did it all start, and how did it get so bad?

The Black Death began in Asia, and the story goes that it came to Europe through Italian ports. The town of Kaffa in Crimea was under siege by Mongols infected with the plague. The army spread the disease to the besieged city, and Kaffa was devastated. (Some argue that this was done purposely as the first act of biological warfare.) Ships fled the dying city, landing in Italian ports, and by the time the Italians realized what those ships carried, it was too late. The plague had arrived, and from Italy, it spread across Europe, rapidly reaching all the way to Scotland by 1350.

Just why was it so hard to stop the spread of plague, though? Plague is a disease originally carried by rats and passed to humans through flea bites. In the 1300s, lack of public and private hygiene meant there were plenty of rats and fleas to be had. It is also quite possible that the disease spread from human to human as well, making it even more difficult to stop. Add in the fact that people in this period had no idea what was causing the disease, and you can begin to see why the Black Death marched through Europe unhindered.

If you contracted the plague, your odds were not good. Most people who got the plague were dead within a week. There was no cure and not even an effective treatment to quell the symptoms—and the symptoms were quite horrible. Bubonic plague gave its victims high fever, nausea, and aches. On top of that, it caused extreme swelling of the lymph nodes, giving a person large, oozing bulges called buboes.

Bubonic was not the only form the plague took, though it was by far the most common. Pneumatic (plague that attacked the lungs) and septicemic (plague that got into the bloodstream) were the two other strains. The survival rate for both these types was almost completely nonexistent. Septicemic plague in particular was a death sentence and could cause a person's skin to turn black (due to tissue death) and body parts (like fingers and toes) to fall off.

The plague eventually ran its course, abating by around 1351, but the damage was irrevocable. Survivors were left in a very different world. For the first time, the demand for workers was higher than the supply, and workers had bargaining power. The plague also eliminated the strict differences between the rich and poor in brutal fashion. The plague was an indiscriminate killer, and it revealed that there was little difference between those at the top and bottom of society. With so many deaths, there was also a surplus of goods, causing prices to plummet. The standard of living for survivors went up because of these things.

It would take time, but the feudal system began to collapse in on itself because of these changes. This was the beginning of the end for the Middle Ages.

The Peasants' Revolt

Change, however, is rarely welcomed by all. As you can imagine, the elites were not too happy about many of the changes brought about by the Black Death. They did not want to pay their workers more, so a law was passed to create a wage ceiling. It did not make the people happy, and their discontent grew.

With the Black Death having run its course, England and France got back to the important business of fighting each other. Richard II took over the conflict from his grandfather, Edward III, when he became king in 1377. While Edward III and his son (Richard II's father, Edward the Black Prince) had done exceedingly well in the conflict with France,

Richard II did not. The war was going poorly, and this created two problems. It made waging war even more expensive, and it made the people more unhappy with the war.

Losing a war was a guaranteed way to make your subjects very upset with you, and this was because of the way taxation worked. The king collected annual revenue through several streams, but that normal revenue did not include money directly from the people. A king could only tax the people directly in dire circumstances, which included war. What the king thus had were people unaccustomed to paying taxes every year who knew that their taxes were going to fund a war that England was losing. These people were also discontent because their wages had been fixed. These were all the ingredients needed for England's first popular uprising.

The final straw that started the revolt was the third poll tax issued by Richard II. Richard II had already used this tax to squeeze extra funds out of his people twice, and this came on top of four years of direct taxation in a row. Richard II was squeezing every last coin from his people, and in 1381, tensions exploded.

The revolt broke out in the southeast, led by a man named Wat Tyler. At first, the peasants were off to a great start. They marched toward London and were enough of a threat to secure a meeting with the mayor and king to voice their demands for reform. Their mistake, however, was in thinking that the elites would treat them as equals. Around thirty years had passed since the Black Death began the process of tearing down the feudal system, but not that much had changed. Wat Tyler was killed by the mayor of London at the meeting.

The painting depicts the end of the 1381 Peasants' Revolt. The image shows London's mayor, Walworth, killing Wat Tyler. There are two images of Richard II. One looks on at the killing while the other is talking to the peasants.
https://commons.wikimedia.org/wiki/File:Assassinat_de_Wat_Tyler_par_Walworth_sous_l%27%C5%93il_de_Richard_II.png

You would think that having its leader murdered would have caused the angry mob to erupt and attack the city, but that's not what happened. Somehow Richard II, who in all other areas had proved himself a very incompetent and cruel king, managed to talk down the rebels and get them all to go home, promising to implement some reform.

That reform never happened. Once the rebels were dispersed and no longer an active threat, they were rounded up and punished. England's first popular uprising had accomplished absolutely nothing. It was a grim reminder that society still had a very strict social hierarchy. The breakdown of feudalism was not going to result in a society where everyone was equal.

Despite not accomplishing anything, the Peasants' Revolt of 1381 is still an extremely important event. It showed that England's lower classes were beginning to have a sense of their rights and power. True rights for the people were still a long way off, but 1381 was the first time the people had even tried to demand it. Times were changing.

Medieval society was not going to go down without a fight, though. While the Black Death was the catalyst for much of the societal change that began around this time, it would take another type of catastrophe of the man-made variety to get England's nobles to accept such change: The Wars of the Roses.

Chapter 9: The Wars of the Roses

The Wars of the Roses is one of the most famous events in English history, even inspiring writers. George R.R. Martin's Game of Thrones series is based on this event, and Shakespeare wrote a trilogy of plays covering it. However, all this attention also means that the history and later legends and stories about the wars have blurred until it's sometimes hard to tell fact from fiction. Our aim in this chapter is to separate history from mythology and learn just what happened in this turbulent period of English history. Like many historical events, we need to start far earlier than the first battle date to do that. It all began with the death of a king.

Setting the Scene

Henry V took the throne in 1413 following the death of his father, Henry IV. Henry V jumped wholeheartedly into the conflict with France started by Edward III, and unlike Richard II, Henry V's military ambitions made him a popular king. The key difference was that Henry V was winning. Henry V's most famous victory was Agincourt, but he enjoyed other successes as well, earning a reputation as a military genius and turning England into a superpower. Henry V even got himself declared heir to the French throne and married the French princess.

All seemed set for England to rise to an unprecedented height when Henry V developed camp fever during a siege. He died suddenly in 1422, and this was very bad indeed for England. Kings die all the time, of course, but what made Henry V's death so untimely was that his son and heir, Henry VI, wasn't even a year old yet. To make matters even more interesting, Charles VI of France died only about a month after Henry V. Because Henry V had been named the French king's heir, this meant that Henry VI was now king of France, as well.

What do you do when the king isn't old enough to rule? In short, someone rules for him, making decisions on the king's behalf. But then, how do you decide who gets to do that? That's a difficult question, which is why Henry V tried to settle matters on his deathbed. He appointed his uncle (Henry VI's great uncle), Thomas Beaufort, to care for the royal person (although Henry VI's mother Catherine also had a very large role in raising her son). Henry V instructed that his brother, John of Bedford, be put in charge of France and named his other brother, Humphrey, Duke of Gloucester, as *tutela* while Henry VI remained a minor. This title could have meant that Gloucester was simply responsible for Henry VI's education, or it could have given Gloucester the effective regency until Henry VI came of age.

That, however, is not what happened after Henry V died. Gloucester was relatively well-liked, but he did not inspire the confidence necessary to give him sole effective reign over England. Instead, he was given a fancy title with strict powers and limitations. He was still a prime player in the English government, but he would not be handed the reins.

So, who was in charge, then? Strangely enough, legally and technically Henry VI was ruling the country. Instead of naming a regent, the elite of English society (Henry VI's uncles, mother, and others) worked together to run the country in Henry VI's name. Documents were worded as though they had been written by Henry VI, and the king was brought to open Parliament in 1423 when he wasn't even two yet. Thus, England operated under a political fiction in which a council of powerful people ran the country while pretending that Henry VI was making decisions.

While that might seem incredibly weird, it shows that the English were very aware of two facts. One was that for kingship and monarchical government to work, the person of the king had to be respected. England's entire governmental system was designed around the central figure of the king, so to throw that out entirely would have caused the system to collapse. Two, England was in a dangerous position. Henry V's military successes had put England in a very powerful position, but his death left the country vulnerable. To be weak and at the top makes you a prime target. The fiction that Henry VI was ruling in his own name was thus an obvious effort to maintain a strong front and keep the nation together. The fact that no one immediately tried to oust the infant king shows just how committed most of the English nobles were to this front.

Thus was the start of a very precarious situation. When a group of people share ultimate power, eventually someone is going to want more. While the conciliar government was in many ways necessary, it created a situation where many different people were commanding power. It would take a strong king to reign in such a group, and that is not what Henry VI turned out to be.

The Kingship of Henry VI

It's hard to be fair to Henry VI. Becoming king before the age of one is bound to give anyone a very strange childhood. There was immense pressure for Henry VI to take over the reins of government as soon as possible, which undoubtedly resulted in him being pushed into situations he was not ready for, such as his coronation at the age of seven. He was also the first English king to be crowned King of France, and his father, Henry V, was a legend to which Henry VI would inevitably be compared. In hindsight, the burden was so large that there was no way Henry VI could live up to expectations, especially as he had no example, having ascended to the throne without ever seeing his father's rule.

Illuminated miniature of Henry VI of England.
https://commons.wikimedia.org/wiki/File:Henry_VI_of_England,_Shrewsbury_book.jpg

However, there is also little doubt that Henry VI did not appear that interested in ruling. By 1437, he was old enough to rule in his own right, and it was soon clear that Henry VI was not his father. Henry VI was a pious and kind man who preferred to spend his time studying scripture and disliked war and government business. This was not what England needed, though. Since Henry V's death, the country had faced setbacks in France and was losing a grip on its conquered territory. John of Bedford was dead, and the English desperately needed their young king to take charge if they wished to keep France.

That, however, appeared to be something Henry VI could not do. Not only did he show little interest, even being described as vacant, but the decisions he made showed incompetence. He was simply not an effective ruler, nor did he have much of a spine, and that left room for other men to try to rule through him. The Duke of Somerset emerged as the victor in this political squabbling and shuffling, achieving a place as Henry VI's chief minister and thus the effective ruler of England. Richard, Duke of York, was quite unhappy with this, believing that he should hold that position. It was the conflict between these two and their allies that would eventually lead to war.

Seizing Power

By 1453, England had lost all its land in France, culminating in a final defeat at Castillon. The grand achievement of Henry V had been undone, and his son did not take the news well, falling into a stupor, or waking coma. The weak king became completely catatonic and would remain so for over a year. He was as effective a ruler as he had been when he had first taken the throne as an infant. Once again, England needed to work out some form of government that could operate without the king.

A council was summoned, and Richard of York did not waste his opportunity. He seized power, arresting his rival Somerset and making himself effective ruler of England during Henry VI's illness. For a year, York ruled the country. But then, suddenly, Henry VI got better. Just as quickly as he had seized power, York was thrown from grace as Henry VI backed Somerset over him. It became quite clear to York that he would never have power so long as Somerset stood in the way, and there was only one way to get around this. York raised an army. The wars were about to begin.

Early Stages of the Conflict

Initially, York did not intend to overthrow the king. He intended to remove the "traitors" around the king, the chief of which was Somerset. Although the two sides made attempts to negotiate, violence broke out at St. Albans on May 22, 1455.

That first battle went quite well for the Yorkists, who overran their opponents and captured the king. Taking the king back to London, York seized control of the country. Somerset had been killed in the fighting, and it appeared that York had successfully pulled off a coup. It is unlikely anyone at this stage could have guessed just how long the conflict would continue.

It was Henry VI's wife, Margaret of Anjou, who proved to be York's greatest opponent. She was not prepared to accept York's rule, and she had possession of one very important aspect of power: the heir. Prince Edward had been born in 1453, and Margaret believed she could wield power through him, especially since her husband Henry VI certainly did not seem prepared to defend his throne. When York lost the support of Parliament in 1456, Margaret acted quickly to increase her power, amassing wealth and appointing people she trusted to government positions, including people like Henry VI's half-brothers Jasper and Edmund Tudor, figures we will return to later.

With York out and Margaret consolidating power, there was a possibility that things might still end peacefully. Arrangements were made for talks in 1458. Although these were completed without the eruption of conflict, there was simply too much bad blood between the two sides for things to end well. Margaret and the Duke of York appeared to truly dislike each other, and many people on the royalist or Lancastrian side (so named because Henry VI was part of the House of Lancaster) had lost loved ones in the battle of St. Albans. The country was crackling with tension, and in late 1459, violence began again.

Again, the Yorkists won the initial battle, but this time they could not take advantage of their initial victory. Their second resort to arms had made it clear to many that they were opposed to the royal government, and Margaret, at least, was not prepared to negotiate. Royal forces, which greatly outnumbered the Yorkists, prepared to engage at Ludlow, and the Yorkist leaders, sensing inevitable defeat, fled to save their own lives, leaving their army to surrender and hope to be spared. Four years after York had so successfully seized power at St. Albans, he was on the run.

However, the Yorkists did not intend to stay in exile. Before the end of the next year, they returned, beat the royalist forces, and entered London. This time, though, York was done fighting to be the king's right-hand man. Now York was declaring himself king.

This was a shock to both his allies and enemies. Since the death of Henry V in 1422, every effort has been made to maintain the position and authority of the monarch, but York had had enough. With Queen Margaret opposed to him and in control of the heir to the throne, York had no chance of holding power as long as the future king was against him. The only way around this was to do the unthinkable and overthrow the king. But, although the king himself made no indication that he cared whether he was overthrown, his wife and her allies were not prepared to give in so easily. It would be a long struggle.

The Wars Drag On

These first years show quite neatly what would continue in England for the next three decades. Each side enjoyed victories and defeats, with periods of triumph and exile. As those first four years show, it was not a period of continuous fighting, which is why it is called the Wars of the Roses rather than a singular war. However, violence always seemed to erupt again, partially because the great amount of blood being spilled left little room for forgiveness. No one wanted to come to peaceful terms with the people responsible for the death of their brother or father. England was trapped in a cycle of violence and hate.

The people who started the conflict were not protected from that cycle, either. York died in the fighting in 1460, and his son Edward, who was now the Duke of York, took up his father's cause quite successfully. Edward defeated the Lancastrian forces and was crowned Edward IV in 1461.

That was far from the end of things, though. Edward IV owed his crown to his uncle, Richard Neville, the Earl of Warwick, who had been York's staunch supporter and the military might behind the Yorkist victory. Warwick expected this to mean that he could effectively rule through his nephew, but Edward IV wanted independence. He began making political moves against Warwick, who after being forced to leave the country, teamed up with old enemies, the Lancastrians, who had been biding their time in France.

Edward IV was now in real trouble, and the Wars of the Roses, which had been "off" for around nine years, were on again. Edward IV fled the country to regroup, and Henry VI, who had been in confinement in the Tower of London since 1465, was put back on the throne. This stage of the wars came to a head at the Battle of Tewkesbury where Edward IV thoroughly defeated his opponents, killing almost all the Lancastrian leaders. He even had Henry VI murdered because, despite his incompetence as a leader, his mere existence was proving too dangerous for the Yorkist king.

To many, the long conflict thus seemed to be over in 1471. Edward IV had two sons, securing his line, before his death in 1483. With twelve years of peace and most of the Lancastrians dead, the conflict should have been over. But the showdown between the House of York and Lancaster had one final act, and it would prove to be something no one expected.

Richard III and Henry Tudor

When Edward IV died in 1483, the throne passed to his eldest son Edward V, except Edward V never got a chance to claim it. His uncle, Richard, Duke of York, had the young king and his brother sent to the Tower of London. They were declared illegitimate, and Edward V was deposed. Their uncle became Richard III, and the boys were never heard from again.

Portrait of Richard III of England, painted by Barthel II (approximate date from tree-rings on panel). The blackletter text on the frame reads: "Richard(us) Rex terti(us)."
https://commons.wikimedia.org/wiki/File:Richard_III_earliest_surviving_portrait.jpg

Of course, the assumption is that Richard III had his nephews murdered, and it is a plausible assumption. Even though he would later face heavy criticism for these alleged murders, Richard III was never able to produce his nephews again after they disappeared into the Tower of London. If they had been alive, he could have saved himself a lot of grief by producing them; if they had escaped, we would expect them to appear in public to contest their uncle's claims to the throne. The bodies of two young boys were found hundreds of years later under some steps in the tower, and many believe that these were the young princes, though there is no proof that this is the case.

Although Richard III took the throne under suspicious circumstances, his reign nevertheless seemed fairly sure. Thanks to the Wars of the Roses, there simply wasn't anyone left to oppose him. At least there almost wasn't anyone.

One Lancastrian claimant to the English throne was left standing: Henry Tudor. You would be forgiven for wondering who this was, for Henry Tudor had little claim to fame. His father, Edmund Tudor, had been the half-brother of Henry VI (Edmund's father, Owen Tudor, a Welshman, had married Henry V's widow). Henry Tudor's mother, Margaret Beaufort, was the great-granddaughter of John of Gaunt, Duke of Lancaster, one of the sons of King Edward III. He thus had a claim to the throne by blood, but it was dubious at best. Dubious, however, proved to be enough. In 1485, Henry Tudor landed in England with an army prepared to push his claim to the throne, and Richard III prepared to meet him.

The two rivals clashed at Bosworth Field. Richard III had superior military experience and seemed confident of a victory over the young would-be king. The battle was decided by the men, not their leaders, though, and in this Henry Tudor proved superior. His forces won the day, and Richard III was killed in the fighting. Thus died the last Yorkist claimant to the throne.

With his victory, Henry Tudor became Henry VII, starting not only a new dynasty but a new era in English history. To cement his rule, he married Edward IV's daughter, Elizabeth of York, finally uniting the two warring houses. The Wars of the Roses were finally over, but there would be lasting changes. The English nobility had been largely wiped out in the decades of infighting, and with them went the last of the old feudal structure. The Middle Ages were ending, and the early modern period had begun.

Chapter 10: The Tudors and the English Reformation

The Battle of Bosworth began a new stage in English history. The Plantagenets, who had ruled England for 331 years, were all dead. All the land in France had now officially been lost (except for Calais). The old feudal system was collapsing. Henry Tudor was taking over a country that had been a mess for the past three decades. Would he be able to restore England to its former glory?

Henry VII

Henry VII has the unfortunate legacy of having been a very effective and capable ruler who was nonetheless not well-liked. His decision to marry Elizabeth of York to combine the houses of York and Lancaster shows some of his political acumen, but his skills were much greater than that. A very hands-on ruler, Henry VII managed his kingdom himself, doing everything from creating policies to managing funds. The consensus is that he did a pretty good job. From the time Henry VII took the throne in 1485 to his death in 1509, he managed to correct quite a few problems the previous English kings had faced.

Likely because of the Wars of the Roses, Henry VII carefully avoided making extremely powerful nobles. He handed out lands and titles sparingly, and while he listened to counsel, he did not rely on only a few powerful men. This refusal to play or promote favorites did not earn

Henry VII many friends, but it prevented the creation of super-powerful and competing nobles that could start another conflict like the Wars of the Roses.

However, this did not mean Henry VII had no uprisings or rebellions to worry about. Having been acquired on the field of battle, Henry VII's position, especially at the start of his reign, was precarious. A king who earns his kingdom through conquest can easily be overthrown by the same means, and there were several attempts. Twice, Henry VII would find himself dealing with imposters claiming to be either Edward V or his brother Richard (the princes who were likely killed in the Tower of London). There were other Yorkist rebellions as well, but Henry VII managed to quell them all. He was not the pushover that Henry VI had been. Henry VII meant to reestablish the strength of the Crown.

Another way Henry VII strengthened royal authority was by getting the royal finances in order. Unlike many kings before and after him, Henry VII lived strictly within his means, relying on the money generated by his lands to run the government and his household. While this was theoretically how kingship was supposed to work, the constant warfare of the past 200 years had caused many English kings to need far more revenue than they were producing, which led them to greatly tax their people. By not going to war, Henry VII saved a good deal of money. He also found ways to acquire more land, which increased his personal revenue. The result was a full treasury.

While Henry VII's policies were no doubt efficient, as we have already mentioned, they did not make him well-liked. Turning the royal revenue around required being extremely strict about collecting fees and stripping lands from some. The constant rebellions also made Henry VII an extremely suspicious and hard man. It can easily be argued that this is what was required of anyone hoping to be a successful king in the wake of the Wars of the Roses, but the difficulties of his situation did not make Henry VII's exacting and distrustful nature easier to bear. Thus, while he was extremely capable, England did not grieve much when he died in 1509. The nation and nobles looked forward to the reign of his more genial son, Henry VIII.

Henry VIII

Henry VIII was the second son of Henry VII and thus did not expect to be king until his elder brother Arthur died unexpectedly in 1502. To secure an alliance with Spain, Henry VIII then married his older brother's betrothed, Catherine of Aragon, an incident that would become extremely important later in his reign.

Portrait of Henry VIII (after 1537). Oil on canvas. Walker Art Gallery, Liverpool by Hans Holbein the Younger.
https://commons.wikimedia.org/wiki/File:After_Hans_Holbein_the_Younger_-_Portrait_of_Henry_VIII_-_Google_Art_Project.jpg

Before we dive into the numerous wives for which Henry VIII is most famous, let's take a moment to understand a bit more about what Henry VIII was like as a king. While his father had been cold and calculating and deeply involved in carrying out government, Henry VIII struck a very different chord as a king. Instead of running things himself, Henry VIII relied more on great men he appointed to run the country for him. That did not, however, mean that Henry VIII was a weak king. He could be incredibly tempestuous, and his councilors, while holding considerable power, only did so at the king's consent. They were often removed almost as quickly as they had risen to power.

One thing that both father and son had in common was an appreciation for the pageantry of royalty. Both Henry VII and Henry VIII knew that looking like a king was an important part of royal authority. They invested in the pomp and circumstance of monarchy, and that investment gave the Tudors an air of legitimacy that helped to cement their rule.

Of course, these traits are not what Henry VIII is remembered for, though. Henry VIII will forever be the king with six wives—and with good reason. Henry VIII's marital troubles would forever change England.

The Wives of Henry VIII and the Reformation

While by his death Henry VIII had been married to six wives, it was the second that caused the stir and changed England. Henry VIII had been married to Catherine of Aragon for two decades when the trouble started, and that trouble was named Anne Boleyn.

This was not the first time Henry VIII had sought a woman other than his wife. His extramarital affairs were well established, but two things made this time very different. First, Anne Boleyn would not become the king's mistress. She wanted to be queen, and she was not going to have sex with Henry VIII unless that happened. Secondly, Catherine of Aragon was now in her forties, which was well past childbearing age for a woman at this time, and she had no son. The only child of Henry VIII and Catherine of Aragon was a daughter named Mary. Even though it was legally allowable, no woman had ever successfully inherited the English throne. The last time one had tried, the result had been a fifteen-year civil war (The Anarchy). These two factors combined made Henry decide to throw off Catherine and marry Anne.

But this was the 1500s, and that was not a simple matter. Divorce was not allowed. Henry VIII needed to have his marriage annulled (to be declared null and void, as though it had never happened), and the only person who could do that was the pope. Except, the pope did not want to help Henry VIII. Rome but the forces of the Holy Roman Emperor, who just so happened to be Catherine of Aragon's nephew, and he did not like the idea of seeing his aunt tossed aside. Catherine was also not prepared to simply step aside. A stalemate ensued that lasted for years, and the entire affair became known as the "King's Great Matter."

If it had been any earlier in history, what happened next would not have been possible, but it just so happened that this occurred in the late 1520s and early 1530s. About a decade had passed since Luther had nailed his Ninety-Five Theses to the church in Wittenberg, sparking the religious tidal wave known as the Reformation. For the first time in Christendom, if Henry VIII didn't like what the pope had to say, he had other options.

That's how, in 1533, the Archbishop of Canterbury, the highest church official in England, annulled the marriage between Catherine and Henry. He then declared the secret vows that Anne and Henry had exchanged a year prior were valid and that the couple was married. This was all done without the pope's approval, sending a clear signal that the English king had turned his back on the Roman Catholic Church, specifically the pope. A year later, in 1534, this was confirmed when the English Parliament passed the Act of Supremacy, which made the king "the Supreme Head of the Church of England." England had officially broken with Rome.

Protestant England?

Since England was no longer Roman Catholic, you might think that made England Protestant by default. While this might be technically true, Henry VIII's Protestant England was a far cry from what was happening in Germany and other hotbeds of the Reformation.

Henry VIII had decided he no longer wanted to listen to the pope, but he still held largely Catholic religious opinions. Although there were ministers in his government who pushed for greater religious changes, Henry VIII kept most things the same. The bishops and archbishops remained but now answered to the king rather than the pope. Catholic doctrinal beliefs also remained intact. For the average person, religious practice in England did not differ much from what it had been before 1534.

Henry VIII made two important changes, however. Henry VIII allowed the Bible to be made available in English and systematically dissolved the entire monastic system in England. It was this second action that caused a bit of an uproar.

At the time of the break with Rome, England had around eight hundred monasteries. Something had to be done with all those Catholic institutions. The immediate response was to attempt to fold them into the new Church of England, but Henry VIII soon saw a more profitable use for the monasteries. The act of supremacy had made the king the Supreme Head of the Church of England, so technically all the monasteries belonged to Henry VIII now. Considering that monasteries owned a quarter of all the used land in England, that was no small gain, and Henry VIII decided to take advantage of it.

In 1536, the first Act of Suppression was passed, which dissolved monasteries with an income less than a certain amount. Dissolving a monastery meant that its land and possessions were taken by the Crown. For the most part, the elite of English society did not bat an eye at this drastic measure. After all, they stood to gain, as much of the monasteries' land would be redistributed among them. The common people, however, took great issue with this step. Monasteries were places of education and relief for the sick and poor. They often played a key role in their communities, so this particular step of Henry VIII's English Reformation was the first to disrupt local life. An uprising called the Pilgrimage of Grace broke out in the north in protest.

Henry VIII was not amused or sympathetic. The Pilgrimage of Grace was crushed swiftly and thoroughly, and the dissolution of the monasteries continued. By 1541, all the monasteries in England had been dissolved. Although it didn't get anywhere, the Pilgrimage of Grace does show that the English people reacted negatively to the sudden religious change forced on them by their king. Changes in the religious beliefs of the whole country take time. It would be many decades after 1534 before England was truly Protestant.

The Other Wives

While none of his other marriages would have quite the impact of Henry VIII's second marriage, it is worth mentioning what happened between Henry and Anne Boleyn and with the rest of his wives to get a better understanding of Henry and his children, who would all rule England.

Despite a successful pregnancy (which could be a rare thing in those days) early in their marriage, Anne did not deliver the much-wanted son and heir, instead only giving birth to a daughter named Elizabeth. Thus, three years after her marriage to the king, she was accused of infidelity, and the marriage was annulled. Two days later, Anne was beheaded, leaving the king to marry his newest infatuation, Jane Seymour. Although we don't know for sure, Anne was likely innocent, and the charges against her were fabricated to get rid of her and leave the king free to marry Jane. It is even more unclear if the scheme was Henry VIII's idea or if he truly believed Anne had been unfaithful thanks to the whispers of members of his court.

It was Jane who finally had the son Henry VIII so craved, giving birth in 1537 to Edward, but childbirth at this time was dangerous. She died twelve days later from complications.

Shockingly, Henry VIII stayed single for three years after Jane's death. His single status represented a great political and diplomatic tool, and his next wife was chosen very carefully. A German princess, Anne of Cleves, was the ideal choice because she was the sister of the Duke of Cleves, who happened to be Catholic but also anti-papal (against the pope). It was a smart alliance for an England that was trying to remain somewhat neutral in the great religious tension of the day.

The marriage was arranged diplomatically, and Anne of Cleves sailed off to marry Henry VIII, who found her repulsive. He went through with the marriage, but when it became clear that he would not start a war by getting rid of her, he had the marriage annulled on the grounds of non-consummation. Although he thought her ugly, Henry VIII did give Anne of Cleves lands and money as a settlement, and she escaped the marriage unscathed, which is more than can be said of his next wife.

The next woman to have the hand of Henry VIII was the Catholic Catherine Howard, an English noblewoman. Her time as queen from 1540 to 1542 saw a brief resurgence of Catholic power at the English court, but Henry VIII soon grew suspicious after having to put down several Catholic plots in the north. Catherine Howard was found guilty of adultery and, like Anne Boleyn before her, beheaded.

In 1543, Henry VIII married his last wife, Catherine Parr, a widow with Protestant sympathies. She outlived her husband and was by all accounts a good wife, good queen, and even a good stepmother to Henry VIII's three children: Mary, Edward, and Elizabeth. While Catherine Parr might not have had as exciting a story as Henry VIII's other wives, she was the only one who kept her marriage to the king intact.

By the time of his death, Henry VIII had accomplished something rather unique. He had had twice as many wives as children (not counting illegitimate children), and all three of his children would eventually reign over England. The children of Henry VIII turned out to be the last of the Tudor dynasty. With the break with Rome still fresh, England was on a journey of religious transformation, and each of Henry VIII's children's reigns would be shaped profoundly by their attempts to direct that religious change.

Chapter 11: Elizabeth I

When Henry VIII died in 1547, his son, Edward, succeeded him despite being the youngest of the children. Edward VI was only nine when he became king, but his health was poor, and his reign ended with his premature death in 1553.

Without another obvious male heir, Henry VIII's eldest child, Mary, managed something that no woman before her had ever done: she became Queen of England. Mary was the first queen to rule England in her own right. She was queen because she ruled England, not because she was married to a king. While that alone is an impressive feat, it can hardly be said that Mary's reign was a success. By the time she died in 1558, Mary had earned the immortal nickname "Bloody Mary." History would not remember her fondly.

Henry VIII's middle child, who came to the throne last, ruled the longest. Elizabeth succeeded her sister in 1558 and ruled until her death in 1603. As Elizabeth's reign was seven to eight times longer than those of her siblings, we will devote most of this chapter to England under Elizabeth I. But before we dive into what many considered to be a golden age for England, let's look more closely at the reigns of Edward VI and Mary.

Religious Settlement and the Children of Henry VIII

Both Edward VI and Mary's legacies revolved largely around how they handled England's religion. Although Edward VI was young, he held much deeper Protestant convictions than his father, Henry VIII. Under Edward VI, England began taking much larger strides toward Protestantism. With changes to things like the prayer book used in worship service, England experienced religious change that could be felt by the common people daily, and this did cause some backlash, such as the Prayer Book Rebellion in 1549.

Despite the resistance of some of the common people, Protestantism pushed forward resiliently under Edward VI, thanks largely to his ministers. Men like John Dudley, Earl of Northumberland, carried out the young king's wishes with what many would call severity. It seemed like a good policy. Edward VI was young, so a man who could please him could expect a long and powerful political career. Only, when the young king died in 1553, the fortunes of individuals and the country radically changed.

Edward VI had no male heirs, which meant the obvious person next in line for the throne was his older sister Mary, but Edward VI's ministers attempted to stop Mary from taking the throne. Mary was firmly Catholic, which did not look good to the people who had just helped Edward VI push England toward Protestantism. They attempted to install Lady Jane Grey on the throne instead. However, Mary acted quickly to gather support, and it soon became clear that the country preferred her to Jane. Mary became queen.

Mary may have secured her throne neatly, but the rest of her reign did not follow that promising beginning. She was determined to see her country return to what she considered the true faith—Roman Catholicism—and to accomplish that, she made a few errors in dealing with her people. Mary, ignoring the warnings of her counselors, married Philip of Spain, a Roman Catholic monarch who insisted on being a co-monarch rather than a consort. The English people did not like having a Catholic foreigner ruling them, and the marriage sparked a brief rebellion. Mary, still determined to return her people to Catholicism, then made herself even more hated by burning many Protestants at the stake as heretics. It was this action that immortalized her as Bloody Mary.

Queen Mary Tudor by Antonis Mor.
https://commons.wikimedia.org/wiki/File:Maria_Tudor1.jpg

Ultimately, though, burning people at the stake was a pretty normal practice in this time of religious upheaval. Elizabeth I would even be guilty of the same (burning Catholics, in her case), so why does Mary have such a bad reputation? History is written by the victors, and if you didn't know already, Mary failed to restore England to Catholicism. She died in 1558, and her Protestant sister Elizabeth took the throne, sealing England's religious future. The now Protestant nation would not fondly remember the queen who tried to return them to Catholicism, and Mary's image was certainly not helped by the immensely popular book by John Foxe, the *Book of Martyrs*, which detailed the deaths of Protestants under Mary, forever making her a villain.

Thus, when Elizabeth I took the throne, she was dealing with a country that had experienced quite a bit of religious whiplash in the last few decades, and her solution to the problem reflected her political acumen. Elizabeth I's religious settlement was decidedly moderate. While she returned England to Protestantism, she also firmly resisted the efforts of the more radical Protestants, namely the Puritans, to instill larger religious changes. For the Puritans, the Church of England far too greatly resembled the Catholic Church, but that did not bother Elizabeth I. Her church struck a middle ground that, although it certainly didn't make everyone happy, seemed to please enough people to stop any violent conflict from breaking out, which was more than could be said for the rest of Europe in the sixteenth and seventeenth centuries.

Elizabeth I - The Pelican Portrait by Nicholas Hilliard.
https://commons.wikimedia.org/wiki/File:Nicholas_Hilliard_Elizabeth_I_The_Pelican_Portrait.jpg

England and Spain

Religious problems were not the only thing that Elizabeth I had to contend with in her forty-four-year reign though. This was the time of both the Renaissance and the Age of Exploration. Writers like Shakespeare were penning plays that would become some of the bests known works of English literature, and explorers like Francis Drake were sailing unknown waters. England vied with other countries to take its place in a rapidly expanding world.

One of England's greatest triumphs in that contest was undoubtedly the defeat of the Spanish Armada in 1588. Although her sister had married Philip II of Spain, Elizabeth did not have a good relationship with the Spanish monarch. Besides the tensions caused by their differing religions (Spain was Roman Catholic), English privateers (pirates) often attacked Spanish ships to steal gold. While the queen did not officially support such illegal actions, she privately encouraged it. Tensions were high, and when England sided with the Protestant Netherlands in their rebellion against Philip II, who had inherited the crown, Spain considered it an act of war and made plans to destroy England.

At the time, Spain was undoubtedly a more powerful nation than England. It had been one of the first to take advantage of the discovery of the New World and had become wealthy from the resources found there. Thus, Spain had the resources to crush England, and Philip II seemed determined to do that, spending the years from 1585 to 1588 preparing an invasion fleet that consisted of 130 ships and 30,000 troops. There was little doubt that if the Spanish force managed to make landfall, England's army, which was poorly trained, did not stand a chance. However, as any basic map reveals, England is an island, so if the Spanish wanted to conquer it, they first had to land.

The Royal Navy was England's only chance, and even though they were outnumbered by Spanish ships, England's navy was not necessarily outgunned. The English ships were smaller and more maneuverable. When the Royal Navy successfully set fire to the Spanish fleet while it was docked at Calais, it managed to scatter the larger force and use more maneuverable ships to pick off targets. Bad weather made the journey home even worse for the defeated Spanish fleet. The whole thing was a disaster for the Spanish.

Defeat of the Spanish Armada, 8 August 1588 by Philip James de Loutherbourg.
https://commons.wikimedia.org/wiki/File:Defeat_of_the_Spanish_Armada,_8_August_1588_RMG_BHC0264.tiff

As bad as it was for the Spanish, the defeat of the Armada was almost equally as good for the English. They had defeated the sixteenth-century equivalent of a world superpower. England was now confident that it could hold its own in the empire-building game that was developing in Western Europe. The dominance of the seas that England established by defeating the Spanish Armada also proved to be a vital factor in England's dominance and colonization over the next few centuries.

England under Elizabeth I was thus a kingdom growing in strength. Coming off the turmoil of the Wars of the Roses and the great religious change caused by the previous monarchs, Elizabethan England began to establish a firmer place in both Europe and the world. We can assume from this alone that Elizabeth I must have been at least a competent ruler as few countries ruled by an absolute monarch can flourish with an inept ruler on the throne. But what was Elizabeth I really like as queen?

Elizabeth I and Mary Queen of Scots

Perhaps one of the best incidents that highlights what Elizabeth I was like as a queen was how she dealt with Mary Queen of Scots. Mary Queen of Scots (called so partially to distinguish her from the numerous other royal Marys of the time) was Elizabeth I's cousin and, as long as Elizabeth I remained childless, next in line for the throne of England.

Monarchs tend to have interesting relationships with the people in line to replace them, and Mary Queen of Scots certainly made things more interesting for Elizabeth I. The Scottish Queen was a Catholic raised in France and ruling over a very Protestant nation. Her poor choice of husbands (the first of whom was blown up in a scheme that rumors said Mary had a hand in) made her subjects distrust and dislike her even more, forcing her to abdicate and flee Scotland in favor of her son, James VI, in 1567.

Mary fled to England, where her cousin, Elizabeth I, was not exactly happy to see her. Because she was Catholic and next in line to the throne of England, Mary was a natural beacon for discontented Catholics under Elizabeth's rule. Having been in a similar position herself while her sister Mary I ruled England, Elizabeth I was all too aware of what sort of plots and conspiracies could be produced by having her rival so close at hand.

Even with these tensions, Mary Queen of Scots lived in England under the watchful eye of Elizabeth I for eighteen years before things imploded. In 1586, a plot to assassinate Elizabeth I and replace her with Mary was discovered. Elizabeth I had had enough, but she did not want to be known for the murder of her cousin. Even with undeniable proof that Mary had been involved in the plot (a letter was found in which Mary agreed to the plan to kill her cousin), Elizabeth I appeared hesitant. She signed an execution warrant but did not give orders for it to be delivered and carried out. Her secretary of state, William Davison, delivered it for her anyway, and Mary was beheaded.

Elizabeth I was furious, claiming it had not been what she wished, and had Davison thrown into the Tower of London. However, he was later quietly released and even given land and a pension, which suggests that Elizabeth I's hesitancy in killing her cousin was feigned to redirect blame away from herself. If so, it was the move of a politically savvy monarch who understood the importance of reputation. Elizabeth I chose the way she presented herself, a skill that often left both her advisers and rivals guessing and allowed her to maintain firm control of her government.

The Virgin Queen

A final aspect to note about Elizabeth I is that her approach to marriage was the opposite of Henry VIII's. She remained unmarried throughout her long reign. It was an unusual move for a monarch but one that seems to match Elizabeth I's personality and ruling style.

As a queen, marrying would have meant sharing some of her royal power, and, as seen from her conflict with Mary Queen of Scots, that was not something Elizabeth I wanted to do. Her virginity also became part of the reputation Elizabeth I carefully crafted and used to inspire devotion to herself. Like her grandfather and father before her, Elizabeth I manipulated the royal image to consolidate her power and authority.

Her singleness also proved to be a constant political bargaining chip. Elizabeth I might have intended from the beginning to never marry, but she did not present herself as completely against the idea. English elites and foreign notables tried to gain the queen's hand, and Elizabeth I had no problem using those attempts for her own ends. For example, her negotiations with Francois, Duke of Alencon and Anjou, as well as a Catholic, may have delayed war with Spain, giving the Royal Navy more time to prepare for the conflict. Still, the older the queen became, the more worried her advisers became, not about her lack of a husband but about the lack of an heir.

Although there was a succession order based on blood, it was traditional for monarchs to officially name an heir to legitimize that person's claim. For all her good qualities, this was one area in which Elizabeth I could not be moved. She refused to name an heir no matter how much her council begged. Her reluctance may have been due to not wanting to repeat her tangles with Mary Queen of Scots, but it also created a tense situation for her kingdom. Changing monarchs leaves a nation vulnerable to external threats and internal fighting. Not having someone lined up to take the throne only greatly intensifies these problems. By not naming an heir, Elizabeth I was securing her power, but she was also leaving her country open to the possibility of a lot of strife when she died. Since she was not immortal, that day did come. Elizabeth I died in 1603. Who would rule England now?

Chapter 12: The Stuarts

The person next in line to the throne by blood was the son of Mary Queen of Scots, James VI of Scotland (also known as James Stuart). When Elizabeth I's approaching death became obvious, her council decided to back James' claim to the throne.

The transfer from the Tudors to the Stuarts could have gone extremely poorly. James was the King of Scotland, which England had a tense history with, and Elizabeth I had had his mother executed. It was very unclear if England would accept him as their new king, but somehow, the succession went smoothly. In 1603, following Elizabeth I's death, James VI of Scotland became James I of England.

This did not mean that the countries were now united. Scotland and England were still two separate kingdoms with different Parliaments and governments. They just happened to share a king. It was a strange arrangement, and James tried to combine his kingdoms to make ruling easier, but neither side was interested. It would be another century before Scotland and England were unified.

Monarchy in the Early Modern Era

To understand everything that unfolded during the reign of the Stuarts, we must pause a moment and consider the concept of monarchy in this period. A lot had changed since the Middle Ages. Early modern England had a very different understanding of who the monarch was and where their authority came from.

The Renaissance brought a revival of interest in classical ideas, including philosophy. Part of that revival was an interest in the Neoplatonist idea of the Great Chain of Being. There's a lot that could be said about this philosophy, but what you need to know is that this philosophy said that the universe consisted of a natural hierarchy. This meant that social hierarchies were part of the very order of the universe. This idea extended to the monarchy and developed into a belief in the divine right of kings, which suggested that monarchs were divinely appointed by God and therefore answerable only to him. This understanding of monarchy thus represented absolute sovereignty. Monarchs were at the top of the Great Chain and answerable only to God for their actions.

This was an idea many monarchs in Europe bought into during this time, but in England, monarchs were answerable in some ways to another governmental body: Parliament. By the era of the Stuarts, it had become incredibly difficult to run the country without Parliament's approval because Parliament controlled the purse strings. The Tudors had managed this by working with Parliament, using tact and political maneuvering to get what they wanted. The Stuarts, especially James I and his son Charles I, would instead try to bully the group into submission, causing tension that eventually erupted into civil war.

That was where things were headed when James I took the throne in 1603, but it would take several decades for things to get there, and a lot happened in between.

The Gunpowder Plot

Two years after James I took the throne, England experienced a conspiracy that lives on in infamy. The Gunpowder Plot was a conspiracy by a group of Roman Catholics to blow up Parliament using barrels of gunpowder. The plan was to kill not only the king but other English leaders in Parliament that day as well, which would hopefully cause enough confusion for the Catholics to seize the government.

The plot was set to take place on November 5, 1605, but the conspirators were found out, and one of them, Guy Fawkes, was arrested while guarding the very barrels of gunpowder. He was subsequently tortured for information about his fellow conspirators and then executed. Although he was not the leader of the plot, Guy Fawkes became so infamous that the English still burn effigies of him on November 5 every year.

Despite failing, the Gunpowder Plot seared itself into England's culture and conscience. Fear of popery (Catholicism) became rampant, a problem the Protestant government saw no reason to curb. Catholics would be discriminated against for generations. All the Gunpowder Plot had achieved was to turn the country even more against Catholicism and even more Protestant.

James I

James I had been king of Scotland since he was one, and he ascended to the throne of England at the age of thirty-six. He thus had something that almost no monarch has when they take the throne: experience. Unfortunately, that experience did not make James I a good king of England.

James I had several problems as a ruler, and some of them were only partially his fault. He ruled during a time of rapid inflation, and, unlike Elizabeth I, his royal household included his wife and children, who each required their own court. Still, his spending habits only made things worse, and he regularly spent more than the royal assets were bringing in. This contributed to one of his other weaknesses as a ruler: his inability to deal with the English Parliament.

While Scotland had a Parliament, it was a relatively weak body that did not leave James I well-equipped to deal with the more headstrong and powerful English Parliament. As a strong believer in the divine right of kings, James I had no idea how to manage a group that thought it had the right to tell him what to do. Even if the Tudors had also believed in their divine right to rule (and they probably did), they were far more tactful than James in how they addressed Parliament. James' solution was generally to avoid dealing with them (going as long as ten years without a full meeting) and find other ways to raise money. Trying to rule without Parliament was a practice his son would also take up with disastrous consequences.

James I did not just clash with Parliament, though. He angered the members of his court by blatantly playing favorites. His attitude and treatment of several young men at court sparked controversy, and the debate about whether these relationships were sexual continues today. However, even if the relationships were sexual, this was not why many disapproved of James I's companions. The king tended to give these men money and power even when they displayed complete incompetence.

For instance, one of James' favorites, George Villiers, the Duke of Buckingham, was allowed to negotiate a marriage between the Spanish princess and James I's son, Charles. Not only did most of the English object to this because they hated Spain and did not want a Spanish princess who would eventually become queen, but Villiers' negotiation strategy also involved sneaking off to Spain with Prince Charles and trying to infiltrate the palace to see the princess. While it may have seemed romantic, the trip accomplished nothing, and the marriage did not happen, much to the relief of the English people.

Thus, James I's reign could hardly be called a great success. He had managed to greatly increase royal spending and tension with Parliament. Still, he made it to the end of his reign without that tension exploding, dying in 1625. His son would not be so lucky.

A Bad Start

Charles I by Anthony Van Dyck.
https://commons.wikimedia.org/wiki/File:Van_Dyck,_Sir_Anthony_-_Charles_I_-_Google_Art_Project.jpg

When Charles I took the throne, he had a problem similar to his father's—namely, the Duke of Buckingham. On their escapade to Spain, Villiers had managed to gain influence over Charles, and it wasn't long into his reign before this had consequences. Since he had been unable to arrange a marriage with Spain, Villiers was now convinced that England needed to go to war with the Catholic nation, a sentiment that already existed in Parliament. Just before James I died, Parliament voted to give the Crown funds to conduct the war. When the king died shortly after, Charles I was left to run the war with Buckingham by his side, of course.

The war was a complete disaster. Taxes spiked to pay for it, putting great strain on the English people. Martial law was implemented in some places, and people had to feed and house soldiers. Even with these extreme measures, there were no military successes.

Someone had to take the blame for all of it. Parliament tried to impeach Buckingham, but Charles I, instead of letting his favorite take the fall, as kings had always done, tried to take the blame himself. While that might seem noble, it was an extremely poor choice. The government and the country rested on the king's shoulders. By admitting to making mistakes, he was destabilizing everything on which the government rested and opening the door to the idea that the king could be blamed for things and held accountable. If that wasn't drastic enough, Charles I then dissolved Parliament to stop it from impeaching Buckingham.

This couldn't last, however. Parliament had to be called again when Buckingham managed to start another war with France (while the war with Spain was still going on). This time Parliament would not vote to give the king more money to fund his wars until he agreed to the Petition of Right, which guaranteed certain protections like not being able to implement martial law on civilians. The fact that Parliament demanded the king sign such a document shows how much trust had been lost between the monarch and his people. Charles I was being asked to sign this document because he had (in the eyes of many) abused his authority. This happened in 1627, only two years after he had become king. It was not a good start.

Ultimately it was not Parliament but a lone assassin that rid the country of Buckingham. He was stabbed to death by a disgruntled officer. Unfortunately, Charles I's rule did not improve with the death of Buckingham.

Worsening Tensions

By 1629, Charles I and Parliament were once again at odds. On March 2, in a rather dramatic scene, the speaker was forcibly held in his chair by some members of Parliament so that the House could pass three resolutions before the king dissolved Parliament. (Sessions of Parliament end when the speaker rises from his chair.) These resolutions were that anyone who paid impositions (import duties paid to the monarch), advised their collection, or pushed religious changes was an enemy of England.

Why were those three things such a big deal? Why would members of the House have held down the speaker to pass these resolutions? These three things were a direct attack on Charles I. It was he who had started impositions to generate money for his wars. To be fair, Charles I did not invent impositions. Other monarchs, including the much beloved Elizabeth I, had implemented them. But Charles I raised them to the point that merchants felt the financial demand was unjust, and Parliament sided with the merchants. Charles I had also married a Catholic wife (albeit for good political reasons) and was cracking down on Puritans (a Protestant sect with a voice in Parliament), whom he believed to be revolutionary and dangerous. Thus, in passing these resolutions, Parliament was saying outright that the king had done wrong. This was a step beyond even the Petition of Right because Parliament had not forced Charles I to agree to the resolutions. Parliament, through its own power, had condemned the king.

Needless to say, Charles I was not happy with this turn of events, and his counter to Parliament's condemnation showed a stubbornness that would ultimately become his fatal flaw. Charles I did not call another meeting of Parliament for the next eleven years. Whether he intended to do this from the start in 1629 or a resolution to not call Parliament happened gradually, Charles I ruled England from 1629 to 1640 without Parliament, a period that became known as the Personal Rule.

Before we get into how people reacted to this, how was it even possible for Charles I to rule without Parliament? Parliament approved new taxes, and it's extremely difficult to run a government without taxes. If Charles I wanted to get away with not calling Parliament, he had to find a way to finance his government without them. In the face of his strained finances, Charles I made some serious changes. He ended the wars with France and Spain and let his treasurer reform his court and government to cut costs.

Both methods proved quite effective in reducing government expenditure. However, cutting costs alone was never going to be enough to solve Charles I's financial issues. He still needed money, but without Parliament, where was he to get it?

The first thing Charles I did to raise money was to completely ignore Parliament's resolutions of 1629. The impositions that Parliament had so thoroughly condemned were raised again. That alone was nowhere near enough to get him the kind of revenue he needed. Other measures soon followed. He sold government offices and monopolies. He had his officials search the law books for any fees and fines technically still on the books that he could use to get money from his subjects without new taxation. Fees for things like hunting in royal forests and enclosing land were revived. Old taxes, such as the ship money tax paid by some coastal towns, were extended to the entire kingdom.

As you can imagine, these methods did not make Charles I very popular, but they turned out to be fairly effective. Charles I had enough money to run the country without Parliament, but it was never a situation that could last. Tax strikes soon began, and the local gentry Charles I had to rely on to collect these taxes often participated in the strikes themselves. England simply did not have a governmental bureaucracy that could operate without the consent of the upper tiers of society. Barons and earls effectively ran the government in their local areas, so without their help, Charles I could not make his people pay up. Thus, by 1640, his government was barely financially afloat.

The Tipping Point

As much trouble as Charles I had with the English Parliament, it was not England that caused the Personal Rule to eventually erupt. Like his father before him, Charles I was king of both England and Scotland. Ruling two distinct kingdoms as a single monarch was undoubtedly tricky, but in trying to make his kingdoms more similar, Charles I vastly underestimated the religious devotion of the Scots. In 1637, when Charles I tried to impose the Anglican English Book of Common Prayer on the Presbyterian Scots, the northern country, which was notoriously divided, united against the king. By 1638, the Scots had signed the National Covenant declaring their opposition to the king's religious policies and stating that only the Scottish Parliament and Presbyterian General Assembly could make religious policy for Scotland. They were telling the king in no uncertain terms to stay out of their business.

Charles I could not ignore such an act of rebellion, not if he wished to maintain his authority. He raised an army to combat the rebellious Scots in the First Bishops' War. However, without money from Parliament, his army was poorly funded. Even worse, the English did not appear to care about helping Charles I crack down on his northern kingdom. Not only did they hate the Personal Rule, but many Englishmen (especially Puritans) sympathized with the Scots and their resistance to Charles I's religious policies. Charles I could not trust such a reluctant army. He instead made a truce with the Scots to buy time until he could raise money to fund a better army.

After eleven years, the king finally called Parliament again, but it was short-lived. The body had no intention of giving the king money for an army till he listened to their demands, and he, having no intention of listening to their demands, dissolved Parliament quickly, having accomplished nothing.

War with the Scots broke out again (the Second Bishops' War), and Charles I's forces were beaten and dispersed, allowing the Scots to occupy the north. Once again, Charles I was forced to sign a treaty, but it was only a temporary truce. He had to pay the Scots a large sum each day to maintain the peace (money he did not have). Unless Charles I found money to pay off the Scots and raise another army to deal with them, the Scots could simply march into London whenever they chose. Whether he liked it or not, Charles I had to talk to Parliament.

Chapter 13: The Civil Wars and the Protectorate

Things were only going from bad to worse in Charles I's reign, but the boiling point had not yet been reached. With the Scots on his doorstep, Charles I again called Parliament late in 1640. This time, Parliament would not be dismissed or disregarded so easily.

A Country Divided

In 1640, Charles I's popularity hit its lowest point. Almost all of Parliament was against the king, and now that Charles I had called Parliament, thanks to the impending threat of the Scots, the body quickly began passing legislation to show its displeasure. The passed acts said Parliament could not be dissolved without its consent, the king must call Parliament every three years at the least, and that taxation not approved by Parliament was illegal. None of these things could become law without Charles I's signature, but, desperate for money, he agreed to everything.

Why would such a stubborn king agree to sign acts that were intended to strip him of power? It's pretty simple. He never intended to let Parliament get away with it. All Charles I needed was the money to deal with the rebellious Scots, and then he could set about undoing everything Parliament had done to limit his sovereignty. In his mind, Charles I was completely justified in such a plan. Because he believed in the Great Chain of Being (discussed in the previous chapter) and the divine right of monarchs to rule, he viewed Parliament's attempts to restrict him as against the natural order and inherently wrong. To overturn all they had done would simply be to set things right.

Unfortunately for Charles I, the members of Parliament knew their king. They did not trust Charles I to keep his promises, so they continued to postpone giving him the money for his army. They were afraid that after Charles I dealt with the Scots, he would then turn that army on Parliament. Ironically, this delay benefited Charles I. As the Parliament wore on, Parliamentary leaders began passing more and more radical acts to check royal power. There were still many in Parliament with moderate and conservative tendencies, and they began to shy away from the direction the group was heading. When, in 1641, leaders on the radical side tried to pass the Grand Remonstrance, a long list of grievances against the king, Parliament split almost fifty-fifty. It was now clear that, two years after being almost universally condemned, the king still had many supporters.

In this divided atmosphere, the final straw came not from Scotland but from Ireland, which had been under English control since the twelfth century. Rebellion broke out in Ireland, and the native devotion to Catholicism quickly led to violence toward Protestant settlers. Ireland was in an uproar, and the English needed a military to stop it.

But Parliament was still not prepared to hand control of an army to the king and instead tried to appoint its own general. Charles I was furious and tried to arrest five key Members of Parliament, but the House of Commons would not give them up, humiliating the king. Lines had been drawn, and there was no turning back.

Soon after this incident, the king left Parliament and London for York. Two centers of English government now existed, and inevitably they must clash. Both Parliament and Charles I raised forces and armed themselves, not to deal with the Irish rebellion but in preparation for a conflict with each other. When Charles I raised his standard on August 22, 1642, this conflict officially began.

The Civil War

The English Civil War, as the clash came to be known, began very well for the Royalists (supporters of King Charles I, also known as Cavaliers). Parliament, although used to funding wars, simply did not have any experience running the military side of things. It was no match for the king's forces, who had most of the country's military talent on their side.

However, the Parliamentarians (also called Roundheads) did have advantages. They had seized control of London before the war officially began, and with that, they controlled southeast England, which happened to be the wealthiest part of the country and the closest to Europe. The navy had also sided with the Parliamentarians, giving them control of the ports. The Roundheads thus had superior resources and the ability to cut off the Royalists from outside help. If the Royalists wanted to win, they needed to do so quickly.

The first battles looked promising for the Royalists. However, they could not completely overwhelm their opponents, and this proved disastrous. The Royalists failed to take London, which was their best option for putting a quick end to the war. As the war dragged on, the Parliamentarians gained the military experience they had lacked at the outset, and one man in particular began to stand out.

Oliver Cromwell first became a notable figure in the English Civil War in 1644 at the Battle of Marston Moor, where he led a cavalry charge that scattered the Royalist flank. However, the Parliamentarian leadership failed to pursue the losing royal army, so the victory did little toward ending the war. The two sides had both had success at this point, but neither seemed able to push its advantage.

After about three years of indecisive battles, Parliament decided to make some major changes to its military structure, creating the New Model Army, a more centrally structured force with promotion by merit as opposed to the previous local militia-style force with ranking based on blood. Most of the Parliamentarian command was thus replaced, but not the successful Oliver Cromwell, who became the General of the Horse in the New Model Army.

It did not take long for the New Model Army to prove effective. On June 14, 1645, it beat the Royalist forces at the Battle of Naseby in the decisive victory that Parliament had been looking for. A large portion of the Royalist forces surrendered, and the war ended a few months later. The fighting was over, but the peace would prove just as trying.

Cromwell at the Battle of Naseby by Charles Landseer.
https://commons.wikimedia.org/wiki/File:Charles_Landseer_Cromwell_Battle_of_Naseby.JPG

Negotiating with the King

What happens after you beat a king? Parliament had won on the field of battle, but Charles I was still king. The war had not been to overthrow the king but to force him back to the negotiating table. Charles I had lost, and now he would be forced to make some concessions and agree to the winning side's demands. That was what everyone expected to happen—everyone, that is, except for Charles I.

Charles I may have lost the battle of the armies, but he still considered himself the moral victor. He did not believe Parliament had any right to restrict him and adamantly refused to negotiate with them. Not only would the king not reach an agreement with Parliament, but he attempted to negotiate with other groups that had an interest in the conflict, such as the Scottish and Irish, hoping to eventually raise another army and reverse his plight. An agreement between Charles I and Scottish Covenanters caused a brief renewal of violence in 1647 (two years after the Battle of Naseby had ended the war). Negotiations with the king were going nowhere, but many members of Parliament still would not give up on reaching an agreement.

Eventually, it was the New Model Army that decided to end things. It seized control of Parliament and would not allow members who had voted to continue negotiations with Charles I to enter. In these circumstances, many members simply chose to stay home. Thus, of the roughly 200-

member body, only about seventy (known as the Rump Parliament) decided to put the king on trial for treason.

In some ways, this was ridiculous. Treason in a monarchy is betraying the monarch. How could Charles I be guilty of betraying himself? Legally, the Rump Parliament was never going to win a trial based on this kind of reasoning, which is why it instead argued that Charles I was guilty of treason against the English people.

Charles I did not think this was a reasonable argument. He did not even believe that he could be tried for a crime because he was the one who made the laws, and (as the head of the government) all the courts were technically his courts. In his mind, the whole trial was illegal and invalid, so he refused to defend himself during it. It was not a good attitude to take during a trial to determine whether he was guilty of a capital crime. On January 27, 1649, the king was found guilty and sentenced to beheading. On January 30, he was executed.

England had done the unthinkable. In a world where monarchy was the only major form of government in Europe and the right of the king to rule was seen as a divine prerogative, England had cast off its king. What were the English going to do now?

A Commonwealth

Killing the king was a radical step that went beyond simply getting rid of Charles I. To try and execute the king for treason was to attack the office itself. So, it should come as no surprise that by May 19, Parliament had abolished both the monarchy and the House of Lords and named England a commonwealth (a republic).

While this might seem like a natural progression to us today, the fact that it took four months between the death of the king and the establishment of the Commonwealth shows that this was not natural at the time. This was well over 100 years before the American Revolution, and there was hesitancy about trying such a radical government change. Could a commonwealth bring stability when it was throwing off so much?

The concern about stability was far more than political opponents trying to disregard the new republic style of government. It had been seven years since the Civil War started, and the country had descended into quite a bit of chaos during this time. The chaos of civil war only became worse when the war ended, and many common people who had helped

Parliament achieve victory began to wonder why they must stay at the bottom of the social hierarchy. If the king could be toppled, why not the whole structure?

This sentiment led to the formation of many groups with radical ideologies (both political and religious), such as the Levellers (who wanted radical government reforms, such as universal suffrage for males), Baptists (who believed in adult baptism, a radical idea at the time), Diggers (who did not believe in private property), Ranters (who believed everyone could decide right and wrong for themselves), and the Quakers (who believed each person held an inner light, the Holy Spirit, which was to be obeyed above all else). From a twenty-first-century perspective, some of these groups appear more radical than others. Regardless, you can imagine the chaos of so many different ideologies springing up at once and trying to exercise their systems all over a war-torn country. While we might embrace this level of diversity today, in the 1600s, it was the definition of anarchy.

So, what was Parliament, which still consisted only of the people who had executed the king (the Rump), going to do about it? How would Parliament bring stability back to the nation? The Rump ultimately tried to walk a middle ground between radical change and the status quo that left no one happy, and the lack of supporters soon led to the Commonwealth's downfall. This downfall came in the form of the army. The New Model Army had won Parliament its power, but Parliament was eager to disband it. Getting rid of the army would have lowered taxes which is always a good way to win popular support. Unfortunately, the army could not be disbanded because Parliament still owed the men their pay, and the only way to raise the money to pay the army would have been to raise taxes. It was a paradox the Commonwealth couldn't solve.

The Commonwealth tried to prolong dealing with the army by sending it out to pacify Scotland and Ireland, which had chosen to support Charles I's son Charles II's claim. Here the New Model Army was greatly successful, which helped the Commonwealth gain some prestige, but Parliament could not seize advantage of the situation as it had hoped. It was still disliked by most, and when it tried to cut the army's pay, that was the end. On April 20, 1653, Oliver Cromwell entered the Commons Chamber with soldiers and dissolved Parliament. The Commonwealth had promised much but done little. It was time to try something else.

The Protectorate

There was another brief attempt at having another Parliament run the country, but this, too, proved ineffective. In December of 1653, a new government was created with Cromwell, who was by far the most powerful man in the country, as the executive. Avoiding the title of king, he was named Lord Protector, but in power and practice, he was running the country just as a monarch would.

Cromwell's government was in some ways a vast improvement over the other options of the past century. It was efficient and carried out reforms. Even though Cromwell was a Puritan, his government was largely religiously tolerant, leaving many (but not all) of the new religious sects in peace. The Protectorate was far from perfect, though. That effective and large government required substantial funds, so tax rates remained high. Also, during the Protectorate, many Puritans held positions of power and tried to enforce moral reform through legal means, combating everything from gambling to drinking. This was naturally not a popular move with the common people and led to a longstanding and often inaccurate understanding and dislike of Puritans in the English mind.

Whatever his government's flaws, Cromwell showed that he was a capable leader. He ruled England uncontested and managed to bring stability after many years of fighting and political chaos. However, while Cromwell's strong leadership made the Protectorate a viable government, it came with one glaring flaw. How would the government he had established survive without him?

Chapter 14: Restoration and the Union with Scotland

When Cromwell died suddenly of sickness in 1658, his son Richard Cromwell became Lord Protector in his place. This succession made it abundantly clear that the Protectorate functioned like a monarchy in all but name. But if that was so, why have the Protectorate in the first place?

The Restoration and Reign of Charles II

No one seemed able to answer that question because the Protectorate didn't last long without Oliver Cromwell. From the time of Cromwell's death to early 1660, chaos returned, with several failed governments. England, particularly the ruling elite, longed for an end to the constantly changing governments, and there seemed only one way to do that. After eleven years without one, England wanted its king back.

The king in question was Charles I's son, Charles II, who was living in exile on the continent. Calling him back to take the throne was no simple matter, though. England, Parliament particularly, had executed his father. How would Charles II feel about returning? Would he seek revenge on the men and families of those who had killed his father? Powerful people in England had no interest in inviting a king back who would immediately try to chop off their heads.

The situation was tense, but thanks to the advice of a man named Edward Hyde, Charles II managed to create a smooth restoration with a single masterstroke: the Declaration of Breda. This was a public announcement by Charles II that declared a general amnesty, some freedom of religion, the recognition of land settlements that had occurred during the Protectorate, and payment of arrears to the army. More basically, Charles II promised not to chop off the heads of anyone involved with the death of his father and not to take back any land people had gained. He was also offering to do what all the previous government had failed to do and pay the army. The Declaration of Breda offered the nervous Parliament a clear olive branch, and Parliament jumped to take it. Charles II entered London on May 29, 1660. England once again had a king.

But what exactly had changed? England was so eager to restore order that it accepted Charles II back without making any provisions to prevent what had happened with Charles I. After fighting a civil war and functioning without a king for eleven years, England appeared to have nothing to show for it.

While the changes might not have been immediately obvious, the turmoil of the past decades had changed a lot. The English government needed both Parliament and king, as attempts to rule without both had resulted in tyranny and chaos. Still, it was unclear which of these had the ultimate sovereignty. The king's powers were largely restored to what had been before the Civil War, but he did have to agree to the reforms that the Long Parliament had made in 1641 (such as calling Parliament at least every three years). Parliament also voted Charles II a much larger annual income than they had given his father, recognizing the king's need for adequate funds to run his government. Compromises had been made, and a settlement had been reached. Unfortunately, it didn't last.

At first Charles II seemed like exactly what England needed. He was charming, intelligent, and, unlike his father, flexible and willing to compromise. However, it eventually became clear that, like his father and grandfather, Charles II believed in the absolute authority of the monarch. Over his reign, he worked to whittle back the restrictions placed on him by the settlement. However, the new king was also rather lazy. He did not have the drive to seize absolute control from a resistant Parliament.

That wasn't the only problem, though. Charles II fought several expensive and largely unsuccessful wars against the Dutch. His need for money to fight these wars drove him to ally with France, which frightened the English people because France was a Catholic superpower. When, in

1672, Charles II tried to do the unthinkable and grant toleration to Catholics with the Declaration of Indulgence, the English had had enough. An angry Parliament refused the Declaration of Indulgence and instead passed the Test Acts, which required all officers to deny transubstantiation (a key Catholic doctrine) and take Anglican communion. The king had tried to open things up for Catholics but ultimately caused the door to be shut even more firmly against them.

The fear of Catholicism reached a new height in 1678 when a rumored plot to kill Charles II and restore England to Catholicism became widespread, despite being false. The Popish Plot, as it came to be known, caused the English to revert to an almost hysteric hatred and mistrust of Catholics and popery.

It was this hysteria that led to an event known as the Exclusion Crisis. The Whigs (an emerging political party with its origins in the Parliamentarian side of the Civil War) attempted to have Charles II's brother, James (who was next in line for the throne since Charles II had no legitimate heirs), excluded from the succession. Their reasoning was quite simple: James was Roman Catholic.

To exclude James from the succession, the Whigs needed to gain a Parliamentary majority and then pass legislation. With the English population almost rabid with its fear of popery, the Whigs won this majority quite easily in two elections. But, both times, Charles II managed to protect his brother by dissolving Parliament before it could pass the bill. This led to many protests and petitions, but Charles II did not back down, dissolving a third Parliament before it could exclude his brother.

Surprisingly, this delay tactic worked. The Whigs slowly lost their momentum, becoming more desperate and radical. In 1683, a plot was discovered (it is unclear how serious the plot was) to kidnap and kill both Charles II and his brother. This was all the ammunition the royal government needed. Radical Whigs were suppressed, and the Exclusion Crisis was over. In this last great test, Charles II had proved triumphant. When he died two years later in 1685, he left his brother a crown that was in an extremely strong position politically and financially. However, James II was still a Roman Catholic.

The Glorious Revolution

It had been over 100 years since England's last Catholic monarch (Mary Tudor, nicknamed Bloody Mary). Since then, England had become Protestant in more than name, and its dislike of anything stinking of popery had grown to levels of intense hatred and fear. In some ways, James II didn't stand a chance.

James II by Godfrey Kneller.
https://commons.wikimedia.org/wiki/File:King_James_II.jpg

Besides his religious convictions, was there anything wrong with James II as a king? During the reign of his brother, James II had served in the military and was a capable soldier. He was orderly, bringing an efficiency to the royal government that his pleasure-loving brother had lacked. While he was Roman Catholic and believed that England should return to what he considered the true faith, he pursued policies of religious toleration rather than trying to persecute Protestants.

However, James II had several flaws. His love of order made him a strong proponent of strict hierarchy. Like his beheaded father, James II did not like to be questioned. This attitude, combined with a strong sense of conviction, led to a monarch who doggedly pursued removing restrictions against Catholics even though most of his people were against such steps. The anti-Catholic sentiment ran so deep in England that James II faced a rebellion against his rule the same year he took the throne (1685). He put down the rebels without any difficulty, but it was not an auspicious start to his reign.

It did not take long for things to unravel, and the issue ultimately came down to a matter of heirs. When he took the throne in 1685, James II already had two daughters: Mary and Anne. They were both Protestant. As long as one of them was the heir, the throne would pass safely back into Protestant hands, and James II's reform attempts would come to nothing.

James II's first wife, Anne Hyde, had died in 1671, and he had remarried a Roman Catholic, Mary of Modena. Thus, when Mary of Modena became pregnant in late 1687, Protestant England became very nervous. If she gave birth to a boy, the Protestant eldest daughter Mary would be skipped in succession, and the throne would pass to a boy who was almost certain to be raised Roman Catholic.

In the summer of 1688, the worst happened. A prince was born. The issue of a Catholic heir was so controversial that James II invited a myriad of witnesses to be present for the birth to confirm its legitimacy. Many of the Protestant witnesses, however, found reasons to look away, and for many years there were rumors that the prince had been smuggled up in a warming pan after the queen gave birth to a stillborn child. This rumor was unfair and no doubt disheartening to the proud parents, but its persistence shows just how loathsome many in England found the idea of a Catholic heir. A Catholic king they could maybe endure. A Catholic dynasty, though, was unbearable.

It was thus the birth of the prince, named James after his father, that sparked one of the most unusual revolutions in history. Three days before the birth, the situation had become so tense that seven of the most powerful men in England wrote a letter to William of Orange, inviting him to invade.

Just who was William of Orange, though, and what stake did he have in England? William of Orange was the leader of the Dutch Republic and a major Protestant leader in the religious wars of this time. (He greatly opposed the expansion of the French Catholic empire.) He was also married to James II's eldest daughter, Mary, the heir to the throne of

England until the birth of the prince. For England, William was the only way they could ensure the throne passed to Mary and out of Catholic hands. For William, England was a much-needed resource and ally in his fight against France. He accepted the invitation to invade, landing in England on November 5, 1688.

James II did not acquit himself well in what followed. Essentially, he panicked and hesitated when he needed to act decisively. He had the resources to beat back the invasion, but he lacked the confidence. Maybe he didn't trust his people, who so clearly disliked him, or maybe he couldn't forget the fate of his father, Charles I. Whatever the reason, the more James II hesitated the more supporters he lost. When even his daughter, Princess Anne, left the court, it became clear James II was on his own. Without even meeting William in battle, James II fled the country, and William and Mary became King and Queen of England.

William of Orange Landing in England by Hoynck van Papendrecht.
https://commons.wikimedia.org/wiki/File:William_of_Orange_III_and_his_Dutch_army_land_in_Brixham,_1688.jpg

The fact that James II fled the country rather than be officially beaten became a point of contention in future days. There were those (known as Jacobites) who thought James II and his descendants were the rightful holders of the English throne. These sentiments proved particularly strong in Scotland and Ireland and would lead to conflict later.

However, the revolution that replaced James II with William and Mary was itself relatively bloodless. The very bloody Civil War had occurred less than five decades before, making this revolution seem almost easy. It became known as the Glorious Revolution, and it was the last time an English monarch would lose the throne.

Union with Scotland

As kings, the Stuarts didn't have a great track record, but the dynasty still had a few monarchs left. Mary, the daughter of James II, was now queen, but it was her husband William's influence that shaped England more directly in the years following the Glorious Revolution.

William's goal, as mentioned earlier, was to stop France from turning Europe into a Catholic empire, and now that he was King of England, he expected the English to do their part in this very expensive conflict. He saw England as a major power that was crucial to the fight.

The English did not see it that way. What happened on the continent seemed remote to their island, but William was nothing if not determined. England found itself involved first in the Nine Years' War, which ended in 1697. Shortly after the conclusion of this war, France violated the treaty that had ended the war by trying to unite Spain and France into a single empire. War broke out again in 1701, and while William was ready to once again lead the charge against France, he never got the chance, dying following an accident on horseback in 1702. The throne passed to the only remaining Protestant Stuart: James II's youngest daughter, Anne.

England was at war with France, and Anne was the last Stuart. While these facts might seem wholly unconnected with Scotland, they would lead to a union that James I had failed to achieve when he became king of England. To understand just how, we need to establish the context.

Although Anne was married, she had numerous failed pregnancies and no surviving children. That meant when she died there would be no direct heir, and her closest living relative was Prince James, the Catholic son of James II. After everything they had gone through to get rid of James II and his Catholic heir, England was not simply going to accept Prince James. Parliament passed the Act of Settlement, which settled the succession on Anne's nearest Protestant relatives, the descendants of James I's daughter Elizabeth, who would become the Hanover dynasty.

The solution seemed simple enough, but there was a problem. The Act of Settlement was legislation passed by the English Parliament, and although Scotland had the same queen, it had a separate Parliament. Scotland did not approve of the Act of Settlement and instead passed the Act of Security, which stated that after Anne's death, the Scottish Parliament would elect her successor in Scotland. There was little doubt as to whom they would choose: Prince James.

England did not like this. Not only would they have a northern neighbor with a king who thought he was the rightful heir to the English throne, but it was also likely this would result in Scotland reviving its old alliance (known as the Auld Alliance) with France, with whom England was currently at war. There was only one clear way to stop this from happening. The two kingdoms had to be united.

How would this happen, though? James I had tried, but both the English and the Scottish were against it. There was still much tension and resentment between the two countries in Queen Anne's Day. The English thought poorly of the Scots, and the Scots did not want to be absorbed by their southern neighbor. Because of things like the Act of Security and a fear of a resurgence of the Auld Alliance, England was prepared to overlook these tensions to secure Scotland before it could cause trouble. But how were the Scots to be convinced?

Ultimately, money was the motivating factor that made the union happen. By becoming part of the British nation, the Scots would gain access to the English trade empire, which could do much for the northern nation, which was struggling economically. Money also became a factor in less subtle ways. England paid Scotland a flat sum to unite the nations. It is also highly likely members of the Scottish Parliament received personal bribes, as well. England did have to make some concessions to seal the deal, such as agreeing to let Scotland maintain its religious practices (Presbyterianism) and laws. Thus, in 1707, the Act of Union was passed, creating Great Britain.

Union Jack.
https://commons.wikimedia.org/wiki/File:Flag_of_the_United_Kingdom_(3-5).svg

All the Stuarts had been monarchs of both England and Scotland, but it wasn't until the last ruler of the dynasty that the two countries became one. The Stuarts had at one point fractured the nation, but in the end, they managed to make it larger before passing the torch to the Hanovers. In 1714, Queen Anne died. She was succeeded by George of Hanover, the son of Sophia, who was the granddaughter of James VI. A new dynasty had begun.

Chapter 15: Eighteenth-Century Britain: Expansion, Wars, and Revolutions

English history until this point has been focused largely on the monarchs because, as a monarchy, England's course was shaped by the decisions and personality of its ruler. However, as we saw in the last several chapters, the power of Parliament had been steadily rising. England remained a monarchy and technically remains one today, but the monarch would come to have less and less real power as the Hanover dynasty progressed.

Instead, Parliament and political parties gained greater and greater influence on the direction of the country. By this time, two parties had emerged, the Whigs and the Tories. These parties had emerged after the English Civil War, with the Whigs coming from the Parliamentarian view and the Tories the Royalist side. The ideas of the two parties changed greatly over time, but it was still these two parties dominating Parliament as the eighteenth century began.

It isn't just monarchs and political parties that shape a nation, though. Larger forces and movements cause events and impact a country and its people. Eighteenth-century England was home to one of the most significant movements in history, an event that would forever change how people lived in England, Europe, and the entire world. This is the time of the Industrial Revolution.

The Industrial Revolution

In truth, to call the Industrial Revolution an event is not historically accurate. The Industrial Revolution refers to the process in which a country's economy becomes focused on factory rather than domestic production. It happened gradually over time, and in England, the time frame of that change was around the eighteenth century, particularly the second half.

Why the eighteenth century, and what caused the Industrial Revolution now in England's history? The simple answer is technological advancements. Many industries were impacted by new technology that made the production of goods faster and possible on a mass scale. The textile industry provides a great example. Inventions like the spinning jenny (a machine that could spin multiple threads at once) and the water frame (a spinning machine powered by a water wheel), both from the 1760s, made it possible to spin thread at a rate and scale completely unmatched by hand laborers.

Spinning Jenny from Museum of Industry.
https://commons.wikimedia.org/wiki/File:Mule_Jenny_Industriemuseum_Gent.jpg)

The machines were one thing, but another important advancement that made the Industrial Revolution possible was the discovery of different sources to power those machines. With steam and coal powering their machines, factories could produce goods nonstop and at a constant rate.

There were other factors at play besides technology, though. A growing population created a workforce that could meet the high demand for labor required by the massive increase in business. This increase in population also came at a time when agricultural production had increased due to technological advancements, so fewer workers were needed for food production. For the first time in human history, most of the population did not need to be farmers, opening the possibility of an economy centered on the production of factory goods.

The mass production of goods during the Industrial Revolution made the economy boom, but it also drastically altered the structure of society. The machines that made such mass production possible were expensive and big, requiring someone with the initial capital to build a factory and start a business. The production of goods thus moved out of the homes of skilled laborers and into factories owned by manufacturers. As the number of factories grew, laborers who produced things by hand were forced out of business and moved to urban areas to get jobs in the factories. The demand for labor was so high that those who did not traditionally earn a wage, such as women and children, found themselves at work in the growing number of factories. Thus, from about 1750 to 1880, England went from being a primarily agricultural society with a spread-out population to an industrialized society with an increasingly urban-centered population.

New layers were added to society, as well. As industry increased, wealth became less tied to land. A new class of industrialists emerged who held great wealth without being members of the traditional landed gentry. The wealthy were not the only ones affected, though. The growing urban population and large number of factory workers created a more politically conscious people, leading to things like unions and eras of reform. Of course, much of the reform that was demanded was due to the terrible working conditions that the Industrial Revolution also produced.

The Industrial Revolution didn't just impact people in England. It also impacted England's place in the world. The wealth that industry brought would prove instrumental in allowing England to dominate the globe over the next 200 years. Economics alone, however, were not enough to turn England into a global superpower. In the eighteenth century, a country's fate was closely tied to its military might.

Establishing Dominance

During the eighteenth century, England was involved in several armed conflicts, including the War of Spanish Succession, the War of Austrian Succession, the Carnatic Wars, the Seven Years' War, and the American Revolution, and this list is far from exhaustive. Not only was England involved in other conflicts in this century, but most of the wars listed were made up of many separate conflicts. For instance, during the American Revolution, England was at war with the American colonists, but Spain, France, and the Netherlands all took the opportunity to take a shot at England as well.

But why are the wars of this century so complicated? The eighteenth century was a time of intense competition between the European powers. Spain, France, the Netherlands, and England were all competing to build overseas empires connected through trade. War broke out frequently around the globe as different countries vied for control of new areas, trade routes, and more. Alliances were forged and then broken. Many groups besides the four nations mentioned above became steeped in various conflicts. It was a high-stakes and complex game of colonization and conquest, and England (Great Britain by this point because England, Wales, and Scotland had been united) would come out as a pretty clear winner by the end of the century. There is no room to even begin to discuss all these conflicts here, but we can at least get a brief understanding of some of the major ones and their consequences for England.

The War of Spanish Succession (1701-1714)

After fighting the Nine Years' War to prevent the growth of the French empire, one of William of Orange's last acts as the King of England was to bring the nation into another war to prevent French imperial ambitions. Although William died shortly after, England stayed in the war, fighting alongside many allies to prevent France from uniting the Spanish and French empires.

England did very well militarily in this conflict, largely thanks to the military mind of John Churchill (a distant ancestor of Winston Churchill). However, despite the victories, the war dragged on until Parliament had grown sick of fighting and sought a peace settlement. The war was ended by the Treaty of Utrecht, which gave Great Britain new territories, a monopoly on the slave trade, and more. While some saw this as a small victory, these strategic gains would prove crucial for England's empire-building.

The War of Jenkins' Ear (1739-1748)

This strangely-named conflict began when a ship captain named Jenkins presented Parliament with his ear, which had allegedly been cut off by the Spanish after they boarded and pillaged his ship. The incident took place in the West Indies (modern-day Caribbean), which the English and Spanish had been fighting over since the days of Queen Elizabeth. England was already unhappy with the Spanish over this area, so the incident of Jenkins' ear was enough to spark a war.

The War of Jenkins' Ear soon became part of the larger conflict of the War of Austrian Succession. Because of its absorption into the larger war, which involved many more countries, there was no clear ending to the conflict between Spain and Britain. The War of Austrian Succession was ended by the Treaty of Aix-la-Chapelle, which was negotiated largely by France and Britain. Although the treaty settled a lot of things, it notably did nothing to settle the colonial disputes between France and Britain, which had become the two superpowers. The failure to address these disputes led directly to the next war on our list.

The Seven Years' War (1756-1763)

Trouble was brewing between France and England, as they both sought to become the dominant colonizing power, and it finally broke out in the American colonies, of all places. A dispute over possession of the Ohio Valley, a border area between French and British-controlled areas, led to bloodshed in 1754, and by 1756, the dispute had escalated into a truly global conflict, with fighting in the Americas, India, and Europe and many other nations becoming involved.

With several different fronts and seven years of fighting, there is no space here to dive into the military history of this war. What you should know is that by the end of the war, Britain had come out on top. The war was ended by the Treaty of Paris in 1763, which gave Britain most of France's holdings in North America and India. Britain also gained Florida from the Spanish. With this victory, the British Empire was secure and expanding.

The Carnatic Wars

The Carnatic Wars were a series of conflicts throughout the eighteenth century in India. These wars were fought over control of the coastal Carnatic region of India. Both France and Britain were involved, seeking to support different claimants to the area. Britain ultimately won control of the area through the Treaty of Paris that ended the Seven Years' War.

What is interesting about these wars and revealing about this period is that, at times, the wars were fought by a company. The forces of the English East India Company wanted to ensure that they had a monopoly on the region's resources and trade. Colonization and trade had brought so much wealth to Europe that companies were able to act with powers normally restricted to governments. This would not last as, in the nineteenth century, the English government stepped in, breaking the company's monopoly and taking political control of India.

The American Revolution (1775-1783)

While it may come as a shock to many Americans, the American Revolution was not one of the key conflicts of the century for Britain. However, it is one of the few that Britain lost, and that does make it an interesting case study.

While the conflict was mainly over the American colonies' desire for independence, like other wars in this century, the American Revolution became more complicated. Spain and France, seeing an opportunity to hurt their rival, joined the colonists against Britain. At the same time, Britain was fighting a separate war with the Netherlands, which was also supporting the colonists. In this time of competition, no conflict was off limits as a chance to weaken rivals for imperial power.

Thanks largely to the help of France, as well as the colonists' perseverance and what can only be called military errors by the British, the colonists won their independence from Great Britain. The unstoppable juggernaut had been defeated, but how big of a deal was this for the British Empire?

While Britain had tried to prevent the loss of the American colonies and the loss was devastating, it was not to be a crippling blow to the empire. The wealth and power that Britain had built up over the century could not be overthrown with a single loss. Furthermore, trade between the new United States and Britain resumed shockingly fast, allowing

Britain to continue to reap economic benefits from its former colonies. The American Revolution showed simultaneously that Britain was not unstoppable and that its status as a world power could be shaken but not undone. However, the American Revolution did not leave Britain unscathed, and perhaps the worst blow was dealt to King George III and the monarchy.

Internal Changes

For a long time, King George III has taken the brunt of the blame for the loss of the American colonies. The popular narrative of American independence claims that George III was a tyrant whose lust for power pushed the Americans to revolution. As with many simple explanations of history, this understanding fails to capture the nuance of what exactly went wrong in George III's reign. The king was less a tyrant and more sadly incapable of handling the complex political problems that arose during his reign. George III was king during a time of emerging popular politics when the opinions of the people were beginning to be manipulated as a political tool. It was also a time of political instability when control of Parliament was uncertain.

King George III proved unable to manage these problems. He picked his ministers poorly, leading to accusations of favoritism and a desire to restore royal prerogative. He supported Parliament and his ministers even as they made decisions that pushed the American colonies closer and closer to revolution. Once the war had begun, the king made things worse when he stubbornly insisted on continuing the fight to retain the colonies even after it became apparent that Britain was losing. Although many historians now believe, based on the evidence, that these actions were made by a king who believed strongly in his duty to guide the nation rather than a tyrant, it does not change the fact that George III often made poor decisions. By the time the American colonies had been lost, Parliament and England had little faith in its king.

George III did gain some competence as he gained experience. He successfully engineered the emergence of the government of William Pitt the Younger, but in doing so, he ensured his own increasing irrelevancy. Although the king had helped Pitt the Younger rise, both knew George III could not manage his political opponents without Pitt. This left most of the power in Pitt's hands. The prime minister was the real force of the English government.

This change in the power of the monarch only became more entrenched when George III became mentally ill. It is now believed by many that the king had porphyria, a condition that caused the excessive production of certain compounds in the blood, poisoning the entire nervous system. While this exact diagnosis cannot be confirmed, it remains undoubtedly true that George III suffered from mental illness. In the late eighteenth century, he suffered only a bout of insanity, but in the last decade of his life (from 1811 to 1820), he was mentally unsound with only brief times of lucidity. Although his son, George IV, was named as regent during this decade, the king's mental illness left the government of England almost entirely in the hands of the ministers and Parliament.

Something had changed in the English government. The monarch, who for so long had been the government itself, could for the first time be seen as a figurehead. George III wielded real power (even late in his reign before the mental illness overcame him permanently), but he was the last English monarch to do so. From then on, England was ruled more by its prime minster than its monarch.

Chapter 16: The Union with Ireland

England had grown quite a lot since emerging as a nation back in the tenth century, and part of that growth was its union with Wales (made official under Henry VIII in 1536) and Scotland (achieved in 1707). These three together formed the country known as Great Britain, but there was another part of the British Isles that had yet to be officially incorporated: Ireland.

Thus far in this book we have not explored what was happening between England and Ireland. So, to understand how union with Ireland happened in 1801, we must go back in time and learn a bit more about the relationship between the two countries.

Kings of Ireland?

Wales was conquered by Edward I and then officially united with England under Henry VIII. Scotland became connected to England when James I became king of both nations, with the Stuarts ruling both as separate countries until the union under Queen Anne. Ireland's story is not so straightforward.

England first laid claim to Ireland in the Middle Ages under Henry II. As with Wales, England hoped to gain territory through conquest, but the conquest of Ireland was far from complete. England had secured a foothold in the country but only held control in one area, which became known as the Pale, leaving most of the island under the control of various Irish clans.

The Tudors tried to establish firmer control, but Ireland was too independently minded. Even the Anglo-Irish nobles (English settlers who arrived during the Middle Ages and intermarried with the Irish) who lived within the Pale did not always respect the English Crown. The Reformation then made the situation far worse. Whatever the English may have thought or tried, the Irish had no intention of becoming Protestant. Attempts to convert them only increased Irish nationalism and weakened England's hold.

With conversion making no progress, Elizabeth I tried another method to subdue the stubborn Irish: plantations. By taking lands from Irish Catholics and redistributing it to Protestant English settlers, the queen may have hoped to change the landowning class in Ireland into a group that was more sympathetic and willing to be ruled by England. These Protestant English settlers became known as the New English.

This plan, too, did not work. Giving away their land only made the Irish more resentful. A rebellion broke out in the Northern Ireland region of Ulster in 1594 under the leadership of the Earl of Tyrone. Hence, it became known as Tyrone's Rebellion. Tyrone picked his moment well because the English were engaged in other military conflicts on the continent and unable to devote their full attention to the Irish rebellion. The rebellion dragged on for nine years. A lot of land and property were destroyed, and many civilians died.

Ultimately, the English put the rebellion down, but the scars it caused were deep and bitter, only worsening the relationship between Ireland and England. Many of the Irish nobility fled to the continent in the aftermath, leaving Ulster without a ruling class. England acted quickly, giving the land to Protestant New English settlers. This was the origin of the region that would become Northern Ireland.

Ireland again tried to rebel during the English Civil War. For a while, the Civil War was so hectic that Ireland was left alone, but once Cromwell was in charge, Ireland was brutally brought to heel. The destruction was so great that many who escaped violent deaths later died of starvation.

Decades later, the Irish again saw an opportunity to throw off the English yoke. Unlike the rest of James II's kingdoms, Ireland was rather happy that he was a Catholic. After James II fled England during the

Glorious Revolution, he garnered the support of Irish Catholics to reclaim his kingdoms. He had regained control of almost all of Ireland except for the Protestant-dominated Ulster when William of Orange met him at the Battle of Boyne (1690), where James II and the Irish Catholics were defeated. Once again, Ireland had failed in its rebellion.

William III at the Battle of the Boyne by Jan Wyck.
https://commons.wikimedia.org/wiki/File:King_William_III_at_the_battle_of_the_Boyne,_1690.jpg

The failure of this very Catholic uprising left the Protestant landowners with even more power. They controlled the Irish Parliament and soon passed laws restricting Catholics from doing everything from voting to buying land. Thus, while most of Ireland was Catholic, it was a terrible place to be a Catholic.

Although England had put down rebellion after rebellion, its control of Ireland was still unstable. The repeated subduing of Ireland made its people more and more resentful. England held on to Ireland only through might, and there was very little practical union between the two. How did a political union happen, then?

Ireland in the Eighteenth Century

Ireland going into the 1700s was a split nation. Most of the population was Catholic, but since Catholics were severely restricted, most of the land was owned by Protestants. This meant that the Protestants controlled the Irish Parliament and were making decisions for the Irish.

There was naturally a lot of tension between the two groups. The Protestant landowners rented land to Catholic tenants, but the lack of understanding and cooperation between the groups hindered any economic growth. Protestant landlords tended to spend most of their time in London instead of on their land. This meant that they were more interested in the rental income they could earn than investing in the land itself. To earn as much rent as possible, land was subdivided among as many tenants as possible, often leaving Irish peasants with too little land to make a living with. This problem of subdivision was only worsened by the Irish tendency to divide holdings among sons instead of passing them intact to the eldest as the English did.

All these problems were made even worse by the fact that there was little to do in Ireland other than farm. With no other industries to turn to, the problem of small land holdings increased as the population grew. Agricultural technology did not advance quickly in Ireland either, so the growing population put a great strain on the country. In short, Ireland in the eighteenth century was poor and divided sharply between the ruling elite and the peasant class.

However, a political nationalism that sought greater Irish independence was rising, and the source of that nationalism was shockingly the Protestant landlords. While this powerful ruling minority might not have cared about the rights of Irish Catholics, they cared about themselves and were becoming increasingly annoyed at the direct interference of the British Parliament in Irish affairs. Even though Ireland had a Parliament, the British Parliament often legislated directly for Ireland and made decisions that hurt the Irish. While Ireland saw itself as a separate kingdom with the same king (much as Scotland had been before the union), it was clear that England saw Ireland more like a colonial holding.

Thus, the Protestant Irish began to long for more autonomy, particularly the right of the Irish Parliament to legislate exclusively for Ireland. Late in the eighteenth century, the Irish achieved this for a time.

In 1780, taking advantage of the precarious imperial situation Britain found itself in due to the American Revolution, Ireland demanded free trade and got it (a major achievement considering that Scotland had had to unify with England to get the same). Then in 1782, the Irish Parliament was granted autonomy in Irish affairs. It was ironically a demand similar to what the American revolutionaries had made. However, the Irish made it when England was trying to hold its empire together and was in no mood to fight a repeat of the American Revolution in Ireland.

The elite class of Irish Protestants had what they wanted, but all was still not well. Although Ireland prospered now that it had free trade and the ability to make decisions for itself, most of the nation was still oppressed and unheard. There had been some loosening of the penal laws that restricted Catholics, but they still held no political power. Agricultural development also still lagged, and poverty was rampant in rural areas, where there were eruptions of violence against landowners and their policies. The country was divided not only along religious but also class lines.

These tensions were particularly bad in Armagh, a county in Ulster, where in the 1780s and 1790s, sectarian violence between a Protestant group called the Peep o' Day Boys and a Catholic group known as the Defenders was intense. A major confrontation between the two groups in 1795, called the Battle of the Diamond, caused the formation of a secret Protestant society known as the Orange Society. The Orange Society's goal was to maintain Protestant power in the face of growing demands for greater rights for Catholics.

The Orange Society was not the only society formed in the 1790s in Ireland. There was also the Society of United Irishmen, which was formed in 1791 and inspired by the French and American Revolution. This group was unique in that it did not have a religious affiliation. Its goal was Irish independence and greater voting rights. Over the decade, the group became more radicalized, entering into full rebellion against British rule in 1798. Like the many Irish rebellions before, the 1798 rebellion did not go well for the United Irishmen. It was snuffed out under the military might of England, and the consequences were severe.

To get Ireland under control, a new Act of Union was passed in 1801 that eliminated the Irish Parliament, instead giving Ireland seats in the British Parliament. The stated goal was to strengthen the connection between the two nations, but it was clear that Ireland had been strong-armed and bribed into the union. The Irish Parliament had only had control of Ireland for eighteen years, and now Ireland was more firmly under British control than ever.

The Irish Question

If the British thought a political union would solve their troubles with Ireland, they had sorely underestimated just how deep the divide between the two kingdoms ran. The "Irish question," as the problem came to be known, was a frustratingly unsolvable and constant problem for Britain over the nineteenth century. But what exactly was the question? What were the problems that plagued the Anglo-Irish relationship after the union?

Despite now being a part of the wealthy British Empire, Ireland remained a poor nation with a stagnant economy. There was still much violence between landlords and tenants, and religious tensions, as always, remained high. The union brought added political tensions, as most of Ireland had no say in British (and hence their own) government since Catholics were excluded from Parliament. Ireland remained a poor and violent place, and England had no idea what to do with it.

In the first half of the nineteenth century, a political movement to emancipate Irish Catholics reached the British Parliament. Thanks largely to the work of a man named Daniel O'Connell, Parliament passed the Catholic Emancipation Act of 1829, which allowed Catholics to sit in Parliament and hold government positions. But there was a price to pay to get the British Parliament to pass such an act. Voting rights in Ireland were heavily reduced so that, even though Catholics could now sit in Parliament, few Irish Catholics could vote.

Catholic emancipation was not the only major thing the Irish wanted, though. Repeal of the Act of Union was the next goal, but on this one, Britain was not prepared to give in to pressure. To reverse the union with Ireland would have been for Britain to take a step backward in its empire building, and England saw this as a step toward destroying its position as a world power. No matter how difficult Ireland proved to be, England was not going to let it go without a fight.

The political unrest in Ireland took a major backseat in the middle of the nineteenth century with the outbreak of the Great Famine (also called the Irish Potato Famine). By the 1840s, much of the Irish population, particularly the vast number of poor farmers, had come to rely heavily on the potato as their food source. For some, potatoes were their sole food. Thus, when a blight devastated the potato crops across the country, the results were catastrophic. Around a million people died either from starvation or diseases caused by malnutrition. Over another million people moved to other countries to find work and food. So devastating was the famine that the Irish population has never recovered. Ireland is the only country in the world that has fewer people today than it did in the early 1800s before the famine.

The famine also worsened tensions between Britain and Ireland. The response of the British government to the disaster was inadequate, to say the least. Programs were started to feed the starving populace and then shut down while many were still starving. The fact that Britain was one of the wealthiest nations on earth at the time made the Irish extremely bitter over the lack of aid.

One group that became radicalized by the Great Famine was a movement called Young Ireland. Young Ireland was a group of young journalists who wanted to renew a sense of Irish culture and identity and repeal the union with Britain. The bitterness caused by the Great Famine turned the group revolutionary, and it tried to start an armed revolution in 1848. However, most of the population was still suffering too greatly from the famine to take up arms. It was a short-lived rising, but it would inspire later Irish nationalism and pushes for Irish independence.

Irish Independence

Irish flag.
https://commons.wikimedia.org/wiki/File:Flag_of_Ireland.svg

Over the next several decades, Ireland continued to simmer. IN the time between the Great Famine and World War I, several new political parties and groups with different ideas for Ireland emerged. The Home Rule movement sought to get the British Parliament to pass a Home Rule act that would give Ireland its own Parliament that would be subordinate to the British Parliament. In response to the Home Rule movement arose Unionism, an opposing movement focused in the Ulster area. The Unionists were against Home Rule. Many of them were Protestants who believed that Home Rule would result in a Catholic rule that destroyed the elite position Protestants had enjoyed for so long, especially in the north. There was also a third group: Sinn Féin. Sinn Féin was more closely aligned with the sentiments expressed by Young Ireland. It wanted independence for Ireland, although by 1905, it was operating as a political party within the British system.

The conflict between these different visions for Ireland reached a head during World War I. Militant Irish nationalists seized what they saw as an opportunity to rebel against British rule, declaring the independent Irish Republic on Easter of 1916, but the rebels had picked a bad time. They received no support from the Irish people or the political parties. However, once again Britain responded harshly, further alienating Ireland. The rebellion was put down, but the swift execution of its leaders by the British turned them into martyrs. The British response to the Easter Rebellion pushed the Irish people away from the Home Rule movement and into the arms of Sinn Féin.

Violence again erupted in 1919 after members of Sinn Féin legally elected to the British Parliament refused to go to London, instead sitting in their own Irish Parliament in Dublin. The ensuing Anglo-Irish War was a guerrilla-style war between the British forces and Irish nationalists. By 1921, both sides were sick of fighting. Britain, whose public had grown sick of the violence and atrocities committed in Ireland, finally agreed to let Ireland go. However, the terms were not to everyone's liking.

Through the terms of the 1921 treaty, Ireland became a dominion of the Commonwealth with an independent Parliament that swore allegiance to the British Crown (much like Australia and Canada). To the more radical members of Sinn Féin, who hated England, this was not good enough. They wanted the Irish Republic that had been declared on Easter of 1916. There was even a brief civil war in Ireland over this point immediately following the 1921 treaty, but the dominion status remained.

(Ireland ultimately became a republic in 1949.)

The other point of contention was Northern Ireland. Six counties in Ulster (where Unionism was strongest) were left out of the dominion of Ireland, with the idea that they might be added later (something that has still not happened over a century later). Ireland was finally independent but no longer whole, and the impact of this rupture is still felt today. Northern Ireland has been a hotbed of violence and terrorism between Catholics and Protestants. The wounds of centuries of tension and strife have proven very hard to heal.

Chapter 17: The Victorian Era

As we saw in Chapter 15, by the close of the eighteenth century and the end of George III's reign, Britain had become a nation ruled primarily by Parliament and its ministers. The monarchs tried to hold onto political power, but by the end of the nineteenth century, their role became largely social and ceremonial.

Nevertheless, the monarch who ruled during this final waning of the British monarch's power has become one of the most famous in British history, with a reign long enough to have an entire age named after her. The Victorian age or era, named after Queen Victoria, who ruled from 1837 to 1901, is one of the most iconic periods of British history for its culture and the political and social changes that helped shape a more modern Britain. (Historians generally give the Victorian era broader dates, starting it in 1820 with the death of George III and ending it in 1914 with the outbreak of World War 1.)

Portrait of Queen Victoria of England, Empress Victoria of India
https://commons.wikimedia.org/wiki/File:Queen_Victoria_-Golden_Jubilee_-3a_cropped.JPG

Social Changes

By the Victorian age, the Industrial Revolution had changed the social makeup of Britain. Throughout the Victorian age, England would become the first nation to industrialize and urbanize. By World War 1, most of England's population lived in urban areas. This population movement had a profound impact on the social structure of the country.

Urbanization could have spelled serious trouble for the aristocratic or noble class in England. The peers and landed gentlemen that made up the top echelon of society originally had power because of the large amounts of land they owned. In an agricultural society, those who own the land own everything, so as cities became the new centers of wealth and power, what would happen to noblemen and their large country estates?

The boring answer is not much. Many of the landed elite were smart enough to invest in industry, and for a long time, the process of urbanization only increased the value of their land. These landowners also held many of the government positions, so even as the rest of society moved to cities and weren't tenant farmers anymore, the landed class still retained much power. Many of the landed elite also retained a sense of responsibility toward the rest of the society. These paternalistic feelings led many aristocrats to join the conservative political party known as the Tories, who believed that maintaining the social hierarchy in society was for the ultimate good of everyone.

Despite this, the Victorian era was the age of the middle class. The middle class included a large variety of occupations and incomes, from industrialists and bankers to clerks and shopkeepers. The middle class included those who worked for a living but not with their hands. This contrasted with the nobility, who prided themselves on the fact that they did not have to work but inherited their living, and the working class, made up of those who worked with their hands.

The Victorian middle class held to an ideology of hard work and the self-made man. They tended to be individualistic and moralistic, believing that people ought to help themselves and that they had earned their relatively good economic position in life. The Victorian middle class also valued a strict separation of public and private life, leading to the idea that women should be confined to homemaking. Since part of middle-class lifestyle was also having servants, this meant that the middle-class women's role in life was to have children.

These values created the society that we now think of as Victorian. Just as the landed class's attitudes lent themselves naturally to a conservative (Tory) political agenda, the middle class's strong sense of individualism led to the emergence of another powerful political movement: liberalism. Unlike the Tories, who wanted to keep things as they were, the liberals (known as the Whigs) wanted reform. With many of them middle-class men who believed strongly in the value of getting things done, the liberals achieved many reforms during the Victorian era.

Before we dive into some of those reforms and how they changed English society, let's discuss the working class. This was by far the largest segment of the population, but as a group, the working class, as we have dubbed them, did not have a sense of class consciousness like the landed elite and middle class. An aristocrat knew and thought of himself as an aristocrat. A middle-class man was middle class and proud of it. A working-class man, however, was more likely to consider himself a miner, an agricultural laborer, or a domestic servant rather than a member of the working class.

Because of this lack of class consciousness and the fact that they couldn't vote, the working class did not have the political presence of the other classes in this era. Some occupations formed trade unions that sought to protect the workers' rights, but these were technically illegal until 1871 and therefore had little political impact. It was the landed Tories and middle-class liberals who were determining the fate of the nation in Parliament.

The Reform Act of 1832

One of the most significant political acts of the Victorian era came in 1832 when the liberal Whigs were in power. Although members of Parliament were technically elected, the system could hardly be called democratic. Very few men could vote (to speak nothing of women). Parliamentary districts had not been reworked along the lines of the great population shifts caused by the Industrial Revolution, so some large industrial towns had no representatives in Parliament while other dying villages had two members in the House. Then there was the outright corruption. Without a secret ballot, it was easy for landlords to dictate votes to their tenants. In some boroughs (parliamentary districts), the member of the House was effectively appointed by the major landlord. Thus, while Parliament called itself a representative body, it was quite clear it did not accurately mirror the nation.

Now, Parliament had existed this way for quite some time, but what changed in the Victorian era was the rising political consciousness of the people, particularly the middle class. The middle class wanted a say in their government, and thanks to a fear of rebellion spawned by events like the American and French revolutions, the ruling class caved into their demands. The Great Reform Act became law in 1832 and represented the first step toward a more truly representative House of Commons.

By modern standards of democratic representation, the Reform Act of 1832 was a small step indeed. It widened the franchise (nationalizing the voting requirements that had previously varied from borough to borough), but voting was still restricted to men and property owners with a certain amount of wealth. There was still no secret ballot. However, the boroughs were reworked so that the growing towns now had representation, and there was no more outright appointment of members by landlords. In this way, the Reform Act of 1832 accomplished what it set out to do, which was to pacify an increasingly agitated and politically aware middle class. Revolution had been avoided, and the door had been opened for a series of continuing reforms that would eventually change the British system without extreme bloodshed.

The Advent of Darwinism

Political changes were not the only forces moving in Victorian Britain. There were also shifts in the scientific community that would have widespread impacts on the rest of society.

In 1831, a young man named Charles Darwin set sail on the HMS *Beagle*. His five-year journey on that ship would prove to be one of vast scientific impact. It was during this trip that Darwin developed his theory of evolution, publishing his famous book *On the Origin of Species* in 1859.

Darwin's theory initially rocked the intensely religious Victorian society, causing much debate. Strangely enough, though, by the end of the century, many people did not see evolutionary theory as a contradiction to Christianity. Theologians argued that natural selection showed the providence of God in all things and so made peace (at least temporarily) with the scientific theory.

Once religious leaders had found a way to work Darwinism into Christianity, many middle-class Victorians were quick to embrace the theory. The idea of natural selection and the survival of the fittest provided evidence for what many of the middle class already believed: the best will rise to the top. Inequality was not bad. It was simply the result of natural selection in human society. In the British Isles, such an attitude made relief to the poor, such as during the Irish Potato Famine, limited. Across the world, this social Darwinism provided scientific justification for Britain's growing empire.

Imperial Britain

With the rise of the middle class, clamor for political reform, and scientific discoveries, a lot was going on domestically in the Victorian era. However, this was also the era when Britain ruled a global empire. Imperialism became a large part of the British identity for the Victorians.

While imperialism normally brings to mind images of conquering armies (which was certainly part of it), Britain's power was largely economic in the Victorian age. Having directly conquered and established many colonies in the eighteenth century, Britain in the nineteenth century established such economic dominance that strict control was no longer necessary. Britain instead pursued a policy of free trade, allowing its colonies to trade with other nations.

Britain also found that establishing commercial dominance in an area did not require a formal takeover. It was cheaper to open trade routes and allow areas to become economically dependent on Britain without formally annexing the territory. Because of this, Britain's global dominance extended well beyond the boundaries of its formal empire.

Still, the colonies that were officially part of the empire remained important for many reasons beyond economics. Places like Canada proved to be ideal destinations for British emigrants. Australia became a convenient way to get rid of convicts. Some colonies served as important ports for British trade routes, and others acted as military outposts to protect the empire. Britain had thus come to rely on its imperial holdings in many ways, and one colony in particular became central to British success: India.

In the Victorian age, the British situation in India could hardly have been better. Trade with India was a source of economic prosperity, and the Indian army made Britain an Asian power. The Indian army was made up mostly of Indians and paid for by Indian taxes, but it was controlled by the British. Britain thus had enormous power for practically nothing. This strange situation was the result of the actions of the East India Company, which had gradually established dominance in India during the last century. That utter dominance passed to the English government when it took control of India in 1858.

The government was concerned with more than making money, however. The East India Company had cared little for changing Indian culture or social structure, but with the morally staunch middle-class

Victorians now calling the shots, efforts soon began to civilize India. This push from Victorian society began even before the government took over. Christian missionaries were allowed into the country in 1813, and certain cultural practices were outlawed, such as *sati*, which was the practice of a widow burning herself on her husband's funeral pyre.

As to be expected, this push to change Indian culture did not sit well with the Indians. There was a mutiny of the Indian army that spread into a more general rebellion in 1847. There was great bloodshed on both sides, and the relationship between Britain and India was permanently soured. Racism and elitism on the British side increased, and dissatisfaction with British rule grew on the Indian side. Things were not resolved finally until Indian independence in 1947.

British India shows both the allure of the British Empire and its problems. The empire at once possessed both a self-bolstering efficacy, where more territory brought greater prosperity and power, and a self-destructive tendency, where more territory caused greater tension and required more management. By the end of the Victorian era, these two poles were fueling an imperialist snowball that would eventually lead to extreme nationalism and the outbreak of World War I.

Between 1870 and 1914, the territory that formally belonged to the British Empire grew rapidly. As other European nations expanded their colonial holdings, Britain felt pressured to expand even more to maintain global dominance. The increasing size of these empires only worsened tensions, as the colonizing powers began to bump into each other around the globe. At the same time, these worsening tensions made many feel that continuing to expand the empire was the only way Britain could have security. With the rivalry between European powers at an all-time high and the imperial presence of these countries across the globe, in some ways the coming of a global war was inevitable.

British Empire at its peak in 1921.
https://commons.wikimedia.org/wiki/File:British_Empire_1921.png

Chapter 18: World War I and II

As discussed in the previous chapter, there was a growing rivalry in empire-building among the European powers by the turn of the twentieth century. In this tense atmosphere, many alliances were formed. During the first decade of the 1900s, Britain made agreements with France and Russia. Although the written agreements between these three were technically a recognition of the other powers' colonial holdings, they signified an informal pledge to mutual aid, and the three countries became known as the Triple Entente.

But just what was the Triple Entente united against? Germany was the chief concern. Its rising dominance threatened Britain's position as a world power. The rapidly growing German navy added much to this distrust. Britain had been the dominant naval power in the world since the defeat of the Spanish Armada in 1588, and as an island nation, it could not but help see Germany's fleet as a direct threat.

Germany was not alone, though. As a member of the Triple Alliance, Germany had allied with Austria-Hungary and Italy. Although Italy would ultimately not honor this alliance, Germany's support of Austria-Hungary was crucial in turning an event in the Balkans into a world war.

When a Serbian nationalist assassinated the Austrian Archduke Franz Ferdinand on June 28, 1914, the dominoes began falling. A month later, Austria declared war on Serbia, perceiving the assassination of the archduke as a threat from that nation. Germany backed Austria in this, but Serbia was backed by Russia. Thus, when Austria and Serbia went to war, so did Germany and Russia. However, Russia had an alliance with France. If Germany wanted to stand a chance in this war, it needed to knock France out of the fight quickly so it could turn its full attention to Russia, and the fastest way to conquer France was to go through Belgium.

It was the German invasion of Belgium that finally crossed the line for Britain. This was too clear a sign of what Germany intended for Europe, and British public opinion and Parliament quickly united in favor of war. Britain declared war on Germany on August 4, 1914. It was believed then that the war would be quick. No one had any idea just how long and terrible this war would become.

Britain in World War 1

For the British and many others, World War I proved the cruelest form of whiplash. Men who marched off to war full of patriotic zeal and confidence found themselves fighting in muddy trenches and dying by the thousands. Instead of decisive offensives and open combat, this war (especially on the Western Front where Britain was most heavily involved) was a tedious and gruesome stalemate.

The First Battle of the Somme has become a bleak representation of just how terrible the war was. To drive the Germans out of France and thus win the war, Britain and France knew they had to be aggressive. In the Battle of the Somme, they tried to do this. After heavily bombarding the German lines with artillery, British troops attacked on July 1, 1916. They were to cross no-man's-land (the open land between the trenches) and seize the German position. It seemed simple enough, but new military technology like the machine gun made attacking an entrenched position all but impossible. The British troops that tried to cross no-man's-land were gunned down in waves, with 20,000 dying on the first day. The Somme offensive lasted several more months, ending on November 13 after 420,000 British casualties. It had achieved almost nothing and has garnered a lasting reputation as the epitome of the futileness and devastation of trench warfare.

By this point, it had become clear that World War I was not going to be like other wars. This was total war, and it would take the efforts of the entire nation for Britain to wage war. Not only were conscription acts passed to bolster the army, but the government also seized control of industries, distributing resources and the labor supply. There was rationing and even the restriction of holidays. The war was felt by all, especially as the horrendous casualty rates began to impact almost every family in England.

If things were so bleak, how did Britain and its allies win the war? Change began in 1916 after two years of stalemate. The British government changed hands from the leadership of H.H. Asquith to that of David Lloyd George. This change in leadership showed just how dissatisfied the country was with the progress of the war. Lloyd George's government would prove somewhat more effective than that of Asquith's. Lloyd George immediately drastically reduced the size of the war cabinet, which allowed decisions to be made quicker and more effectively. He also managed to solve the food crisis caused by German submarines through a convoy system and food rationing.

Lloyd George's success in these areas was the result of traits that also proved harmful in other areas. Lloyd George had a strong personality, and he was determined to end the stalemate and the war. This action-oriented attitude allowed him to make decisions decisively and pursue a course without getting bogged down in the administrative bureaucracy of government. However, his strong personality was not appreciated by the British military command. There was much distrust between Lloyd George and his generals, and their inability to work together hindered the progress of the war on the active front.

Ultimately it would take something outside of Britain to break the long and tedious stalemate. In April 1917, the United States of America declared war on Germany. With fresh resources and men to bring to the fight, the entry of the United States into the war was what the Allies needed. By November 11, 1918, the war was finally over. But what exactly would peace look like?

The Paris Peace Conference

The peace made after World War 1 has since become infamous. Many would argue that the failures of the peace created after World War 1 led directly to the outbreak of another world war less than three decades later. So, what exactly went wrong with the peace negotiations, and what was Britain's role in it?

The fighting of World War I ended with the armistice in 1918, but it would take a year to negotiate the official peace treaty, and "negotiate" is a generous term for what happened. The Paris Peace Conference involved negotiations and arrangements made between many countries, but only four countries had a say: Britain, America, France, and Italy (although the first three ended up making most of the decisions). Britain's representative was Lloyd George, who found himself caught between France's Prime Minister Clemenceau's desire for revenge on Germany and American President Woodrow Wilson's hopes for a more united and stable world. The other Allies were heeded little and the defeated nations not at all. The resulting treaties were thus destined to do little to achieve any lasting goodwill between the countries.

The most infamous example of this is the Treaty of Versailles, which officially ended hostilities between the Allies and Germany. Not only did the treaty force Germany to give up territory (a normal consequence of losing a war), but Germany also had to admit guilt for the war and agreed to pay reparations to the Allied countries. To the Germans, this added a grievous insult to an already bad enough wound. It was not the grounds for a lasting peace.

Appeasement and the Start of World War II

With the benefit of hindsight, it's easy to see now that the Treaty of Versailles was never going to keep the peace with Germany. It's crucial to remember as we move forward in British history that the people living in the time between the two world wars did not have this benefit. No one knew for certain that another world war was coming, and many people were prepared to do a lot to avoid it.

The trauma of World War I left many nations struggling to right themselves again, and a worldwide economic downturn in the 1930s did not help matters. Germany, suffering under the weight of heavy reparations, felt these difficulties most keenly, leaving the country vulnerable to the influence of someone like Adolf Hitler. Hitler promised the Germans restoration of their former greatness, and with his charismatic speaking ability, Hitler soon had control of Germany.

It became clear throughout the 1930s that Hitler did not intend to abide by the Treaty of Versailles. Germany began the construction of an air force in 1935 and re-militarized the Rhineland in 1936. These were steps that could only be regarded as hostile, but the rest of Europe and Britain were weary of war and unsure of how to respond to Hitler's actions.

In the 1930s, Britain ultimately decided to go with a strategy of appeasement, letting Hitler have his way in the hopes that this would prevent war. The most famous proponent of appeasement was Neville Chamberlain, British Prime Minister from 1937 to 1940. For much of the 1930s, appeasement took the form of simply ignoring Hitler's actions even when he went so far as to annex Austria in 1938. However, appeasement reached a new height (or rather low) when Chamberlain, along with representatives from France and Italy, negotiated the Munich Agreement with Hitler in 1939, handing over part of Czechoslovakia to the Germans. The Czechoslovakian government was not part of the negotiations at all. Appeasement had become more than a matter of ignoring Germany's violations of the treaty and was now a policy of even assisting Hitler to stave off war.

War had been avoided, but Chamberlain and his appeasement policies had opponents. One of the most vocal was Winston Churchill, who called the Munich Agreement "a total and unmitigated defeat." It did not take long for Churchill to be proved right. Hitler soon invaded other parts of Czechoslovakia, blatantly ignoring the Munich Agreement. When the Germans invaded Poland on September 1, 1939, Britain could no longer ignore Germany's obvious intentions. Britain declared war on Germany two days later. France did the same, and World War II had officially begun.

Winston Churchill

Although it might seem strange now, it was not obvious at the start of World War II that Winston Churchill was the man to lead Britain through this crisis. Churchill began his career as a soldier and reporter, making a living from his writings. He entered the political arena in 1900 as a conservative member of Parliament.

Winston Churchill.
https://commons.wikimedia.org/wiki/File:Sir_Winston_Churchill_-_19086236948.jpg

However, Churchill did not stay long with the conservatives. In 1904, he split with his party over a disagreement on free trade and joined the liberals. From there, Churchill's rise in politics was steady. He was a close ally and colleague of David Lloyd George, and by World War 1 had earned himself a position as First Lord of the Admiralty (the government minister in charge of the British navy). That, however, was an uncomfortable place to be. When the Gallipoli Campaign of World War 1 failed utterly, Churchill took the blame. He was left out of the coalition government headed by Lloyd George and, in 1915, left politics to become a soldier again.

But Churchill could not stay away long. He was back in government business by 1917, and from then to 1939, his political career was one of ups and downs with little overall progress. He was a constant but often ignored voice until he turned his attention to Germany. Churchill's constant warnings about Hitler and German aggression only became more accurate throughout the 1930s. By the time war broke out, Churchill looked like one of the only government figures who had seen things clearly. Neville Chamberlain thus appointed him to his old position as First Lord of the Admiralty.

By 1940, the war was swinging in Germany's favor, and Chamberlain, acknowledging his failures, resigned his position as prime minister. A coalition government with members of all parties was formed, and none other than Winston Churchill was at its head. Despite his failures in the past, Churchill seemed to be the man with the energy and drive needed to run a war, and no one doubted his unswerving commitment to defeat Germany. Churchill's wartime leadership of Britain would make him a famous historical figure not only in Britain but across the world.

Britain and World War II

Churchill's commitment to resisting Germany soon showed itself sorely needed as the war did not initially go well for Britain and her allies. The Germans' blitzkrieg strategy, which focused on fast offensives to overwhelm and quickly subdue their enemies, was extremely effective. By late June 1940, Germany had conquered the Netherlands, Belgium, and even France. Britain alone remained to defy the German conquest.

The struggle for Britain was fought largely in the air over two months (August and September) in 1940 known as the Battle of Britain. Germany knew that Britain needed to be subdued, but an invading force would never be successful until Germany controlled the skies. The German Luftwaffe thus set out to gain aerial supremacy over the British Royal Air Force (RAF). The air forces were fairly evenly matched; however, the RAF succeeded in beating off German assaults, and the German plan for a full-scale invasion of Britain was abandoned.

This did not mean that Germany had given up forcing Britain to surrender. The Luftwaffe turned its attention to bombing British cities, particularly London, in the hopes of destroying Britain's morale and forcing a surrender. This period of intense bombing was called the Blitz. Despite the onslaught, Britain held firm for an entire year against Germany. Then, in late June 1941, Hitler's forces invaded the Soviet Union, giving Britain an unlikely ally. Later that year when Japan bombed Pearl Harbor, the United States also entered the war. Britain now had two powerful allies and, with them, real hope of victory.

Victory did indeed come, though it would take four long years of fighting to get there. Throughout the war, Churchill met with US President Franklin Roosevelt and Soviet leader Joseph Stalin to discuss war operations and, as the war ended, the postwar situation. Although Britain continued to play an important role throughout the war in defeating Germany, to Churchill's dismay, his and Britain's position increasingly diminished in the face of the two larger powers. The world wars had so overturned the previous world order that Britain, for the first time in several centuries, found itself removed from the top tier of world power. The United States and the Soviet Union were the new superpowers.

Thus, while World War II was in many ways a triumph for Britain, it also spelled the end of British world supremacy. The total warfare had devastated Britain economically, and its wealth had been at the core of Britain's world dominance. After the war, Britain no longer had the resources or the interest to maintain its empire and lost the remainder of its colonial holdings. India gained independence just two years after World War II ended, and other colonies followed until Hong Kong was returned to Chinese sovereignty in 1997.

Churchill was also shockingly ousted as prime minister after the war. Despite his wartime triumph and personal victory in the election, Churchill's party lost its majority to the Labour Party immediately after the war. The decline of the empire and the success of the Labour Party showed how the era of world wars had changed Britain's attitude. In the postwar world, Britain was a country focused more internally on issues like social reform and economic recovery. Imperial Britain was gone, and from its ashes, the modern United Kingdom would emerge.

Conclusion

While much could be said of English history after World War II, we will end our tour of English history there. From a collection of rival Anglo-Saxon kingdoms occupying just a part of the British Isle to the largest empire in history and the United Kingdom, England's story is one of a slow, great rise and a rapid and inevitable decline.

In its beginnings, England was an unstable land. Constantly invaded by outsiders, no centralized sense of nation or government could develop. It was not until the Anglo-Saxons united against the Vikings that any nation that could be called England emerged. However, that was not the end of foreign invasions. The Norman Conquest of 1066 was the last time England would be successfully invaded and conquered. From that time forward, England was free to develop as its own nation without being ripped apart by external powers. But for many centuries, internal conflicts prevented any lasting stability. The Anarchy, Wars of the Roses, Civil War, and Glorious Revolution all highlight the difficulty in achieving a sense of national unity.

Eventually, though, England had settled much of its domestic strife and began to turn its attention ever more outward in the age of exploration and colonization. Thanks to its naval supremacy and the wealth generated by the Industrial Revolution, England beat out its rivals in the imperial game until it had gained an empire and undisputed world dominance.

Such an empire, however, could never last. The more territory England gained, the more resources it needed to maintain it, and the larger the empire, the more prone it was to internal strife. Weakened by back-to-back world wars, England's economy was no longer a world powerhouse, and its empire soon dissolved. Still, compared to those of other empires, England's fall was relatively mild. While its territory has been drastically reduced, England maintains its position as a stable and influential nation. The existence of the United Kingdom today speaks volumes about England's ability to persevere through the many changes its history has seen.

And even if England no longer dominates the world as it once did, its influence remains felt by people around the globe in many ways. English is the most spoken language in the world today. Trials by jury, which originated in England, spread during the period of colonization and continues in some form in many countries. And, although England can hardly take credit for the invention of democracy, the Magna Carta and the American Revolution are events deeply embedded in the development of democratic governments.

England's impact has also had many less favorable consequences. British imperialism and interference in other regions of the world created tensions that can still be felt to this day. Colonization may have created great wealth for Britain, but it was at the cost of the colonized and has left a legacy of prejudice and exploitation around the world. The great strife with Ireland outlined in Chapter 16 is only one story of many showcasing the extremely tense and complicated relationship former parts of the British Empire have with England.

Whether it is for good or ill, the one thing that cannot be denied is that England has had an impact. The history of this small nation has lessons of relevance for everyone.

If you enjoyed this book, a review on Amazon would be greatly appreciated because it would mean a lot to hear from you.

To leave a review:
1. Open your camera app.
2. Point your mobile device at the QR code.
3. The review page will appear in your web browser.

Thanks for your support!

Here's another book by Enthralling History that you might like

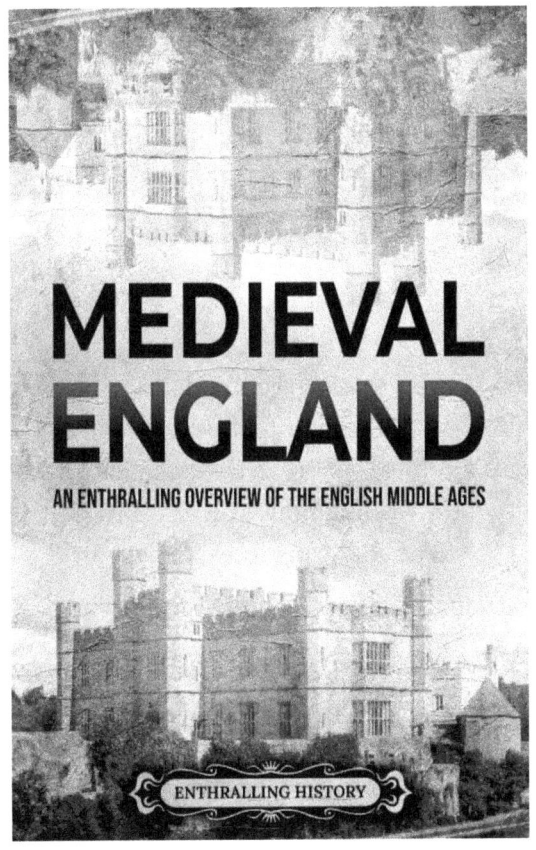

Free limited time bonus

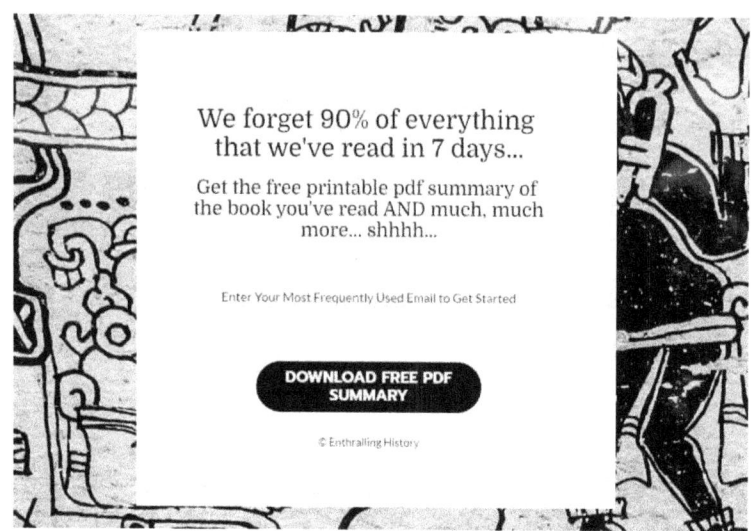

Stop for a moment. We have a free bonus set up for you. The problem is this: we forget 90% of everything that we read after 7 days. Crazy fact, right? Here's the solution: we've created a printable, 1-page pdf summary for this book that you're reading now. All you have to do to get your free pdf summary is to go to the following website:

https://livetolearn.lpages.co/enthrallinghistory/

Or, Scan the QR code!

Once you do, it will be intuitive. Enjoy, and thank you!

Bibliography

Adams, S. "Battle of Edington." Encyclopedia Britannica, April 29, 2023. https://www.britannica.com/topic/Battle-of-Edington.

"An Introduction to Prehistoric England." English Heritage. Accessed June 24, 2022. https://www.english-heritage.org.uk/learn/story-of-england/prehistory/.

Badian, E. "Narcissus." Encyclopedia Britannica, January 1, 2022. https://www.britannica.com/biography/Narcissus-Roman-official.

Blake, R. Norman William and Blake, Baron. "David Lloyd George." Encyclopedia Britannica, August 29, 2023. https://www.britannica.com/biography/David-Lloyd-George.

Brain, Jessica. "King Eadwig." Historic UK, August 27, 2022. https://www.historic-uk.com/HistoryUK/HistoryofEngland/King-Eadwig/.

Brain, Jessica. "The History of the Coronation." Historic UK, May 3, 2023. https://www.historic-uk.com/HistoryUK/HistoryofBritain/History-Of-The-Coronation/.

Breeze, D. J. "Hadrian's Wall." Encyclopedia Britannica, September 1, 2021. https://www.britannica.com/topic/Hadrians-Wall.

Britannica, T. Editors of Encyclopaedia. "Boudicca." Encyclopedia Britannica, December 10, 2020. https://www.britannica.com/biography/Boudicca.

Britannica, T. Editors of Encyclopaedia. "" Encyclopedia Britannica, June 12, 2023. https://www.britannica.com/event/Carnatic-Wars.

Britannica, T. Editors of Encyclopaedia. "Celt." Encyclopedia Britannica, April 25, 2022. https://www.britannica.com/topic/Celt-people.

Britannica, T. Editors of Encyclopaedia. "Declaration of Breda." Encyclopedia Britannica, June 24, 2019. https://www.britannica.com/topic/Declaration-of-Breda.

Britannica, T. Editors of Encyclopaedia. "Decline of the British Empire." Encyclopedia Britannica, October 12, 2020. https://www.britannica.com/summary/Decline-of-the-British-Empire.

Britannica, T. Editors of Encyclopaedia. "East India Company." Encyclopedia Britannica, August 13, 2023. https://www.britannica.com/money/topic/East-India-Company.

Britannica, T. Editors of Encyclopaedia. "Edmund I." Encyclopedia Britannica, May 22, 2023. https://www.britannica.com/biography/Edmund-I.

Britannica, T. Editors of Encyclopaedia. "First Battle of the Somme." Encyclopedia Britannica, October 9, 2023. https://www.britannica.com/event/First-Battle-of-the-Somme.

Britannica, T. Editors of Encyclopaedia. "Industrial Revolution." Encyclopedia

Britannica, August 17, 2023. https://www.britannica.com/money/topic/Industrial-Revolution.

Britannica, The Editors of Encyclopaedia. "Irish Rebellion". Encyclopedia Britannica, 16 May. 2023, https://www.britannica.com/event/Irish-Rebellion-Irish-history-1798. Accessed 18 September 2023.

Britannica, The Editors of Encyclopaedia. "Orange Order". Encyclopedia Britannica, 28 Jul. 2023, https://www.britannica.com/topic/Orange-Order. Accessed 18 September 2023.

Britannica, T. Editors of Encyclopaedia. "Pytheas." Encyclopedia Britannica, December 16, 2009. https://www.britannica.com/biography/Pytheas.

Britannica, T. Editors of Encyclopaedia. "Roman Britain." Encyclopedia Britannica, February 19, 2022. https://www.britannica.com/place/Roman-Britain.

Britannica, T. Editors of Encyclopaedia. "Seven Years' War." Encyclopedia Britannica, August 18, 2023. https://www.britannica.com/event/Seven-Years-War.

Britannica, T. Editors of Encyclopaedia. "Treaty of Aix-la-Chapelle." Encyclopedia Britannica, October 11, 2022. https://www.britannica.com/event/Treaty-of-Aix-la-Chapelle.

Britannica, T. Editors of Encyclopaedia. "Treaty of Versailles." Encyclopedia Britannica, September 5, 2023. https://www.britannica.com/event/Treaty-of-Versailles-1919.

Britannica, T. Editors of Encyclopaedia. "War of Jenkins' Ear." Encyclopedia Britannica, August 1, 2014. https://www.britannica.com/event/War-of-Jenkins-Ear.

"Bog Body: British Museum." The British Museum. Accessed June 24, 2022. https://www.britishmuseum.org/collection/object/H_1984-1002-2.

Bucholz, Robert, and Newton Key. Early Modern England 1485-1714: A Narrative History. 2nd ed. Chichester, West Sussex: Wiley-Blackwell, 2009.

Butser Ancient Farm. Accessed June 24, 2022. https://www.butserancientfarm.co.uk/.

Cartwright, Mark. "Ancient Celtic Torcs." World History Encyclopedia. https://www.worldhistory.org#organization, June 22, 2022. https://www.worldhistory.org/article/1687/ancient-celtic-torcs/.

Cartwright, Mark. "Ancient Celts." World History Encyclopedia. https://www.worldhistory.org#organization, April 1, 2021. https://www.worldhistory.org/celt/.

"Celt (n.)." Etymology. Accessed June 24, 2022. https://www.etymonline.com/word/celt.

Farley, Julia. "Who Were the Celts?" British Museum Blog - Explore stories from the Museum, February 22, 2022. https://blog.britishmuseum.org/who-were-the-celts/.

Heyck, Thomas William and Meredith Veldman. The Peoples of the British Isles: A New History: From 1688 to the Present. 4th ed. New York: Oxford University Press, 2016.

Hingley, Richard. "Julius Caesar in Britain." World History Encyclopedia. https://www.worldhistory.org#organization, July 11, 2022. https://www.worldhistory.org/article/1926/julius-caesar-in-britain/.

Holt, J. "John." Encyclopedia Britannica, March 29, 2023. https://www.britannica.com/biography/John-king-of-England.

Johnson, Ben. "Prehistoric Britain." Historic UK. Accessed June 24, 2022. https://www.historic-uk.com/HistoryUK/HistoryofEngland/Prehistoric-Britain/.

Johnson, Ben. "Roman England, the Roman in Britain 43 - 410 AD." Historic UK. Accessed July 15, 2022. https://www.historic-uk.com/HistoryUK/HistoryofEngland/The-Romans-in-England/.

Jones, Dan. The Wars of the Roses. New York: Penguin, 2014.

"Julius Caesar Invades Britain - 55BCE and 54BCE." mytimemachine.co.uk, May 5, 2016. http://www.mytimemachine.co.uk/?p=5.

"Julius Caesar on Britain - 55BCE and 54BCE." mytimemachine.co.uk, May 5, 2016. http://www.mytimemachine.co.uk/?p=7.

"Julius Caesar on Britain II - 55BCE and 54BCE." mytimemachine.co.uk, May 5, 2016. http://www.mytimemachine.co.uk/?p=9.

Knowles, M. David. "Henry II." Encyclopedia Britannica, July 2, 2023. https://www.britannica.com/biography/Henry-II-king-of-England.

Law, C. M. "The Growth of Urban Population in England and Wales, 1801-1911." Transactions of the Institute of British Geographers, no. 41 (1967): 125-43. https://doi.org/10.2307/621331.

Meigs, Samantha A. and Stanford E. Lehmberg. The Peoples of the British Isles: A New History: From Prehistoric Times to 1688. 4th ed. New York: Oxford University Press, 2016.

Morrill, J. S. and Myers, Alexander Reginald. "Henry VII." Encyclopedia Britannica, July 4, 2023. https://www.britannica.com/biography/Henry-VII-king-of-England.

Myers, A. Reginald. "Edward IV." Encyclopedia Britannica, April 24, 2023. https://www.britannica.com/biography/Edward-IV-king-of-England.

Nicholas, H. G. "Winston Churchill." Encyclopedia Britannica, October 21, 2023. https://www.britannica.com/biography/Winston-Churchill.

Pearson, M. Parker. "Stonehenge." Encyclopedia Britannica, March 2, 2021. https://www.britannica.com/topic/Stonehenge.

Ross, C. "Henry V." Encyclopedia Britannica, November 8, 2022.

https://www.britannica.com/biography/Henry-V-king-of-England.

Small, Andrew. "Why Is Britain Called Britain?" These Islands, December 23, 2017. https://www.these-islands.co.uk/publications/i281/why_is_britain_called_britain.aspx.

Steinbach, S. "Victorian era." Encyclopedia Britannica, October 3, 2023. https://www.britannica.com/event/Victorian-era.

"The Celtic Tribes." The Celtic Tribes - history of Celtic people. Accessed June 29, 2022. https://www.englishmonarchs.co.uk/celts_6.html.

"The Celts of England." Celtic Life International - Celebrating the Celtic Life for over 30 years. Accessed June 24, 2022. https://celticlifeintl.com/the-celts-of-england/.

"The Roman Occupation of Britain." The Roman occupation of Britain. Accessed July 15, 2022. https://sites.psu.edu/romanoccupationofbritain/roman-conquest-of-britain-ad-43/.

"Visit Resource - Prehistoric Britain." British Museum. Accessed June 24, 2022. https://www.britishmuseum.org/sites/default/files/2019-09/visit-resource_prehistoric-britain-KS2.pdf.

Wallace, W. M. "American Revolution." Encyclopedia Britannica, August 27, 2023. https://www.britannica.com/event/American-Revolution.

Watson, J. Steven. "George III." Encyclopedia Britannica, July 3, 2023. https://www.britannica.com/biography/George-III.

Whitelock, D. "Alfred." Encyclopedia Britannica, May 16, 2023. https://www.britannica.com/biography/Alfred-king-of-Wessex.

United States Holocaust Memorial Museum. "The British Policy of Appeasement toward Hitler and Nazi Germany." Holocaust Encyclopedia. https://encyclopedia.ushmm.org/content/en/article/introduction-to-the-holocaust.

"Viking Place Names." JORVIK Viking Centre, March 13, 2023. https://www.jorvikvikingcentre.co.uk/the-vikings/viking-place-names/.